PERSIAN
VOCABULARY

FOR ENGLISH SPEAKERS

ENGLISH-PERSIAN

The most useful words
To expand your lexicon and sharpen
your language skills

3000 words

Persian vocabulary for English speakers - 3000 words

By Andrey Taranov

T&P Books vocabularies are intended for helping you learn, memorize and review foreign words. The dictionary is divided into themes, covering all major spheres of everyday activities, business, science, culture, etc.

The process of learning words using T&P Books' theme-based dictionaries gives you the following advantages:

- Correctly grouped source information predetermines success at subsequent stages of word memorization
- Availability of words derived from the same root allowing memorization of word units (rather than separate words)
- Small units of words facilitate the process of establishing associative links needed for consolidation of vocabulary
- Level of language knowledge can be estimated by the number of learned words

T&P Books Publishing
www.tpbooks.com

ISBN: 978-1-78716-707-0

This book is also available in E-book formats.
Please visit www.tpbooks.com or the major online bookstores.

PERSIAN VOCABULARY
for English speakers

T&P Books vocabularies are intended to help you learn, memorize, and review foreign words. The vocabulary contains over 3000 commonly used words arranged thematically.

- Vocabulary contains the most commonly used words
- Recommended as an addition to any language course
- Meets the needs of beginners and advanced learners of foreign languages
- Convenient for daily use, revision sessions, and self-testing activities
- Allows you to assess your vocabulary

Special features of the vocabulary

- Words are organized according to their meaning, not alphabetically
- Words are presented in three columns to facilitate the reviewing and self-testing processes
- Words in groups are divided into small blocks to facilitate the learning process
- The vocabulary offers a convenient and simple transcription of each foreign word

The vocabulary has 101 topics including:

Basic Concepts, Numbers, Colors, Months, Seasons, Units of Measurement, Clothing & Accessories, Food & Nutrition, Restaurant, Family Members, Relatives, Character, Feelings, Emotions, Diseases, City, Town, Sightseeing, Shopping, Money, House, Home, Office, Working in the Office, Import & Export, Marketing, Job Search, Sports, Education, Computer, Internet, Tools, Nature, Countries, Nationalities and more ...

T&P BOOKS' THEME-BASED DICTIONARIES

The Correct System for Memorizing Foreign Words

Acquiring vocabulary is one of the most important elements of learning a foreign language, because words allow us to express our thoughts, ask questions, and provide answers. An inadequate vocabulary can impede communication with a foreigner and make it difficult to understand a book or movie well.

The pace of activity in all spheres of modern life, including the learning of modern languages, has increased. Today, we need to memorize large amounts of information (grammar rules, foreign words, etc.) within a short period. However, this does not need to be difficult. All you need to do is to choose the right training materials, learn a few special techniques, and develop your individual training system.

Having a system is critical to the process of language learning. Many people fail to succeed in this regard; they cannot master a foreign language because they fail to follow a system comprised of selecting materials, organizing lessons, arranging new words to be learned, and so on. The lack of a system causes confusion and eventually, lowers self-confidence.

T&P Books' theme-based dictionaries can be included in the list of elements needed for creating an effective system for learning foreign words. These dictionaries were specially developed for learning purposes and are meant to help students effectively memorize words and expand their vocabulary.

Generally speaking, the process of learning words consists of three main elements:

- Reception (creation or acquisition) of a training material, such as a word list
- Work aimed at memorizing new words
- Work aimed at reviewing the learned words, such as self-testing

All three elements are equally important since they determine the quality of work and the final result. All three processes require certain skills and a well-thought-out approach.

New words are often encountered quite randomly when learning a foreign language and it may be difficult to include them all in a unified list. As a result, these words remain written on scraps of paper, in book margins, textbooks, and so on. In order to systematize such words, we have to create and continually update a "book of new words." A paper notebook, a netbook, or a tablet PC can be used for these purposes.

This "book of new words" will be your personal, unique list of words. However, it will only contain the words that you came across during the learning process. For example, you might have written down the words "Sunday," "Tuesday," and "Friday." However, there are additional words for days of the week, for example, "Saturday," that are missing, and your list of words would be incomplete. Using a theme dictionary, in addition to the "book of new words," is a reasonable solution to this problem.

The theme-based dictionary may serve as the basis for expanding your vocabulary.

It will be your big "book of new words" containing the most frequently used words of a foreign language already included. There are quite a few theme-based dictionaries available, and you should ensure that you make the right choice in order to get the maximum benefit from your purchase.

Therefore, we suggest using theme-based dictionaries from T&P Books Publishing as an aid to learning foreign words. Our books are specially developed for effective use in the sphere of vocabulary systematization, expansion and review.

Theme-based dictionaries are not a magical solution to learning new words. However, they can serve as your main database to aid foreign-language acquisition. Apart from theme dictionaries, you can have copybooks for writing down new words, flash cards, glossaries for various texts, as well as other resources; however, a good theme dictionary will always remain your primary collection of words.

T&P Books' theme-based dictionaries are specialty books that contain the most frequently used words in a language.

The main characteristic of such dictionaries is the division of words into themes. For example, the *City* theme contains the words "street," "crossroads," "square," "fountain," and so on. The *Talking* theme might contain words like "to talk," "to ask," "question," and "answer".

All the words in a theme are divided into smaller units, each comprising 3–5 words. Such an arrangement improves the perception of words and makes the learning process less tiresome. Each unit contains a selection of words with similar meanings or identical roots. This allows you to learn words in small groups and establish other associative links that have a positive effect on memorization.

The words on each page are placed in three columns: a word in your native language, its translation, and its transcription. Such positioning allows for the use of techniques for effective memorization. After closing the translation column, you can flip through and review foreign words, and vice versa. "This is an easy and convenient method of review – one that we recommend you do often."

Our theme-based dictionaries contain transcriptions for all the foreign words. Unfortunately, none of the existing transcriptions are able to convey the exact nuances of foreign pronunciation. That is why we recommend using the transcriptions only as a supplementary learning aid. Correct pronunciation can only be acquired with the help of sound. Therefore our collection includes audio theme-based dictionaries.

The process of learning words using T&P Books' theme-based dictionaries gives you the following advantages:

- You have correctly grouped source information, which predetermines your success at subsequent stages of word memorization
- Availability of words derived from the same root (lazy, lazily, lazybones), allowing you to memorize word units instead of separate words
- Small units of words facilitate the process of establishing associative links needed for consolidation of vocabulary
- You can estimate the number of learned words and hence your level of language knowledge
- The dictionary allows for the creation of an effective and high-quality revision process
- You can revise certain themes several times, modifying the revision methods and techniques
- Audio versions of the dictionaries help you to work out the pronunciation of words and develop your skills of auditory word perception

The T&P Books' theme-based dictionaries are offered in several variants differing in the number of words: 1.500, 3.000, 5.000, 7.000, and 9.000 words. There are also dictionaries containing 15,000 words for some language combinations. Your choice of dictionary will depend on your knowledge level and goals.

We sincerely believe that our dictionaries will become your trusty assistant in learning foreign languages and will allow you to easily acquire the necessary vocabulary.

TABLE OF CONTENTS

PRONUNCIATION GUIDE

T&P phonetic alphabet	Persian example	English example
['] (ayn)	دعوا [da'vā]	voiced pharyngeal fricative
['] (hamza)	تایید [ta'id]	glottal stop
[a]	رود [ravad]	shorter than in ask
[ā]	آتش [ātaš]	calf, palm
[b]	بانک [bānk]	baby, book
[č]	چند [čand]	church, French
[d]	هشتاد [haštād]	day, doctor
[e]	عشق [ešq]	elm, medal
[f]	فندک [fandak]	face, food
[g]	لوگو [logo]	game, gold
[h]	گیاه [giyāh]	home, have
[i]	جزیره [jazire]	shorter than in feet
[j]	جشن [jašn]	joke, general
[k]	کاج [kāj]	clock, kiss
[l]	لیمو [limu]	lace, people
[m]	ماجرا [mājarā]	magic, milk
[n]	نروژ [norvež]	sang, thing
[o]	گلف [golf]	pod, John
[p]	اپرا [operā]	pencil, private
[q]	لاغر [lāqar]	between [g] and [h]
[r]	رقم [raqam]	rice, radio
[s]	سوپ [sup]	city, boss
[š]	دوش [duš]	machine, shark
[t]	ترجمه [tarjome]	tourist, trip
[u]	نیرو [niru]	book
[v]	ورشو [varšow]	very, river
[w]	روشن [rowšan]	vase, winter
[x]	کاخ [kāx]	as in Scots 'loch'
[y]	بیابان [biyābān]	yes, New York
[z]	زنجیر [zanjir]	zebra, please
[ž]	ژوئن [žuan]	forge, pleasure

ABBREVIATIONS
used in the vocabulary

English abbreviations

ab.	-	about
adj	-	adjective
adv	-	adverb
anim.	-	animate
as adj	-	attributive noun used as adjective
e.g.	-	for example
etc.	-	et cetera
fam.	-	familiar
fem.	-	feminine
form.	-	formal
inanim.	-	inanimate
masc.	-	masculine
math	-	mathematics
mil.	-	military
n	-	noun
pl	-	plural
pron.	-	pronoun
sb	-	somebody
sing.	-	singular
sth	-	something
v aux	-	auxiliary verb
vi	-	intransitive verb
vi, vt	-	intransitive, transitive verb
vt	-	transitive verb

BASIC CONCEPTS

1. Pronouns

I, me	man	من
you	to	تو
he, she, it	u	او
we	mā	ما
you (to a group)	šomā	شما
they	ān-hā	آنها

2. Greetings. Salutations

Hello! (form.)	salām	سلام
Good morning!	sobh bexeyr	صبح بخیر
Good afternoon!	ruz bexeyr!	روز بخیر!
Good evening!	asr bexeyr	عصربخیر
to say hello	salām kardan	سلام کردن
Hi! (hello)	salām	سلام
greeting (n)	salām	سلام
to greet (vt)	salām kardan	سلام کردن
How are you? (form.)	haletān četowr ast?	حالتان چطور است؟
How are you? (fam.)	četorid?	چطورید؟
What's new?	če xabar?	چه خبر؟
Goodbye!	xodāhāfez	خداحافظ
Bye!	bāy bāy	بای بای
See you soon!	be omid-e didār!	به امید دیدار!
Farewell!	xodāhāfez!	خداحافظ!
to say goodbye	xodāhāfezi kardan	خداحافظی کردن
So long!	tā bezudi!	تا بزودی!
Thank you!	motešakker-am!	متشکرم!
Thank you very much!	besyār motešakker-am!	بسیار متشکرم!
You're welcome	xāheš mikonam	خواهش می کنم
Don't mention it!	tašakkor lāzem nist	تشکر لازم نیست
It was nothing	qābel-i nadārad	قابلی ندارد
Excuse me! (fam.)	bebaxšid!	ببخشید!
to excuse (forgive)	baxšidan	بخشیدن
to apologize (vi)	ozr xāstan	عذر خواستن
My apologies	ozr mixāham	عذرمی خواهم

I'm sorry!	bebaxšid!	ببخشید!
to forgive (vt)	baxšidan	بخشیدن
It's okay! (that's all right)	mohem nist	مهم نیست
please (adv)	lotfan	لطفاً
Don't forget!	farāmuš nakonid!	فراموش نکنید!
Certainly!	albate!	البته!
Of course not!	albate ke neh!	البته که نه!
Okay! (I agree)	besyār xob!	بسیارخوب!
That's enough!	bas ast!	بس است!

3. Questions

Who?	če kas-i?	چه کسی؟
What?	če čiz-i?	چه چیزی؟
Where? (at, in)	kojā?	کجا؟
Where (to)?	kojā?	کجا؟
From where?	az kojā?	از کجا؟
When?	če vaqt?	چه وقت؟
Why? (What for?)	čerā?	چرا؟
Why? (~ are you crying?)	čerā?	چرا؟
What for?	barā-ye če?	برای چه؟
How? (in what way)	četor?	چطور؟
What? (What kind of ...?)	kodām?	کدام؟
Which?	kodām?	کدام؟
To whom?	barā-ye ki?	برای کی؟
About whom?	dar bāre-ye ki?	درباره کی؟
About what?	darbāre-ye či?	درباره چی؟
With whom?	bā ki?	با کی؟
How many? How much?	čeqadr?	چقدر؟
Whose?	māl-e ki?	مال کی؟

4. Prepositions

with (accompanied by)	bā	با
without	bedune	بدون
to (indicating direction)	be	به
about (talking ~ ...)	rāje' be	راجع به
before (in time)	piš az	پیش از
in front of ...	dar moqābel	در مقابل
under (beneath, below)	zir	زیر
above (over)	bālā-ye	بالای
on (atop)	ruy	روی
from (off, out of)	az	از

of (made from)	az	از
in (e.g., ~ ten minutes)	tā	تا
over (across the top of)	az bālāye	از بالای

5. Function words. Adverbs. Part 1

Where? (at, in)	kojā?	کجا؟
here (adv)	in jā	این جا
there (adv)	ānjā	آنجا

| somewhere (to be) | jā-yi | جایی |
| nowhere (not anywhere) | hič kojā | هیچ کجا |

| by (near, beside) | nazdik | نزدیک |
| by the window | nazdik panjere | نزدیک پنجره |

Where (to)?	kojā?	کجا؟
here (e.g., come ~!)	in jā	این جا
there (e.g., to go ~)	ānjā	آنجا
from here (adv)	az injā	از اینها
from there (adv)	az ānjā	از آنجا

| close (adv) | nazdik | نزدیک |
| far (adv) | dur | دور |

near (e.g., ~ Paris)	nazdik	نزدیک
nearby (adv)	nazdik	نزدیک
not far (adv)	nazdik	نزدیک

left (adj)	čap	چپ
on the left	dast-e čap	دست چپ
to the left	be čap	به چپ

right (adj)	rāst	راست
on the right	dast-e rāst	دست راست
to the right	be rāst	به راست

in front (adv)	jelo	جلو
front (as adj)	jelo	جلو
ahead (the kids ran ~)	jelo	جلو

behind (adv)	aqab	عقب
from behind	az aqab	از عقب
back (towards the rear)	aqab	عقب

| middle | vasat | وسط |
| in the middle | dar vasat | در وسط |

| at the side | pahlu | پهلو |
| everywhere (adv) | hame jā | همه جا |

around (in all directions)	atrāf	اطراف
from inside	az daxel	از داخل
somewhere (to go)	jā-yi	جایی
straight (directly)	mostaqim	مستقیم
back (e.g., come ~)	aqab	عقب

| from anywhere | az har jā | از هر جا |
| from somewhere | az yek jā-yi | از یک جایی |

firstly (adv)	avvalan	اولاً
secondly (adv)	dumā	دوما
thirdly (adv)	sālesan	ثالثاً

suddenly (adv)	nāgahān	ناگهان
at first (in the beginning)	dar avval	در اول
for the first time	barā-ye avvalin bār	برای اولین بار
long before ...	xeyli vaqt piš	خیلی وقت پیش
anew (over again)	az now	از نو
for good (adv)	barā-ye hamiše	برای همیشه

never (adv)	hič vaqt	هیچ وقت
again (adv)	dobāre	دوباره
now (adv)	alān	الان
often (adv)	aqlab	اغلب
then (adv)	ān vaqt	آن وقت
urgently (quickly)	foran	فوراً
usually (adv)	ma'mulan	معمولاً

by the way, ...	rāst-i	راستی
possible (that is ~)	momken ast	ممکن است
probably (adv)	ehtemālan	احتمالاً
maybe (adv)	šāyad	شاید
besides ...	bealāve	بعلاوه
that's why ...	be hamin xāter	به همین خاطر
in spite of ...	alāraqm	علیرغم
thanks to ...	be lotf	به لطف

what (pron.)	če?	چه؟
that (conj.)	ke	که
something	yek čiz-i	یک چیزی
anything (something)	yek kāri	یک کاری
nothing	hič čiz	هیچ چیز

who (pron.)	ki	کی
someone	yek kas-i	یک کسی
somebody	yek kas-i	یک کسی

nobody	hič kas	هیچ کس
nowhere (a voyage to ~)	hič kojā	هیچ کجا
nobody's	māl-e hičkas	مال هیچ کس
somebody's	har kas-i	هر کسی
so (I'm ~ glad)	xeyli	خیلی

| also (as well) | ham | هم |
| too (as well) | ham | هم |

6. Function words. Adverbs. Part 2

Why?	čerā?	چرا؟
for some reason	be dalil-i	به دلیلی
because ...	čon	چون
for some purpose	barā-ye maqsudi	برای مقصودی

and	va	و
or	yā	یا
but	ammā	اما
for (e.g., ~ me)	barā-ye	برای

too (~ many people)	besyār	بسیار
only (exclusively)	faqat	فقط
exactly (adv)	daqiqan	دقیقا
about (more or less)	taqriban	تقریباً

approximately (adv)	taqriban	تقریباً
approximate (adj)	taqribi	تقریبی
almost (adv)	taqriban	تقریباً
the rest	baqiye	بقیه

the other (second)	digar	دیگر
other (different)	digar	دیگر
each (adj)	har	هر
any (no matter which)	har	هر
many, much (a lot of)	ziyād	زیاد
many people	besyāri	بسیاری
all (everyone)	hame	همه

in return for ...	dar avaz	در عوض
in exchange (adv)	dar barābar	در برابر
by hand (made)	dasti	دستی
hardly (negative opinion)	baid ast	بعید است

probably (adv)	ehtemālan	احتمالاً
on purpose (intentionally)	amdan	عمداً
by accident (adv)	tasādofi	تصادفی

very (adv)	besyār	بسیار
for example (adv)	masalan	مثلاً
between	beyn	بین
among	miyān	میان
so much (such a lot)	in qadr	این قدر
especially (adv)	maxsusan	مخصوصاً

NUMBERS. MISCELLANEOUS

7. Cardinal numbers. Part 1

0 zero	sefr	صفر
1 one	yek	یک
2 two	do	دو
3 three	se	سه
4 four	čāhār	چهار
5 five	panj	پنج
6 six	šeš	شش
7 seven	haft	هفت
8 eight	hašt	هشت
9 nine	neh	نه
10 ten	dah	ده
11 eleven	yāzdah	یازده
12 twelve	davāzdah	دوازده
13 thirteen	sizdah	سیزده
14 fourteen	čāhārdah	چهارده
15 fifteen	pānzdah	پانزده
16 sixteen	šānzdah	شانزده
17 seventeen	hefdah	هفده
18 eighteen	hijdah	هیجده
19 nineteen	nuzdah	نوزده
20 twenty	bist	بیست
21 twenty-one	bist-o yek	بیست ویک
22 twenty-two	bist-o do	بیست ودو
23 twenty-three	bist-o se	بیست وسه
30 thirty	si	سی
31 thirty-one	si-yo yek	سی ویک
32 thirty-two	si-yo do	سی ودو
33 thirty-three	si-yo se	سی وسه
40 forty	čehel	چهل
41 forty-one	čehel-o yek	چهل ویک
42 forty-two	čehel-o do	چهل ودو
43 forty-three	čehel-o se	چهل وسه
50 fifty	panjāh	پنجاه
51 fifty-one	panjāh-o yek	پنجاه ویک
52 fifty-two	panjāh-o do	پنجاه ودو

53 fifty-three	panjāh-o se	پنجاه وسه
60 sixty	šast	شصت
61 sixty-one	šast-o yek	شصت ویک
62 sixty-two	šast-o do	شصت ودو
63 sixty-three	šast-o se	شصت وسه

70 seventy	haftād	هفتاد
71 seventy-one	haftād-o yek	هفتاد ویک
72 seventy-two	haftād-o do	هفتاد ودو
73 seventy-three	haftād-o se	هفتاد وسه

80 eighty	haštād	هشتاد
81 eighty-one	haštād-o yek	هشتاد ویک
82 eighty-two	haštād-o do	هشتاد ودو
83 eighty-three	haštād-o se	هشتاد وسه

90 ninety	navad	نود
91 ninety-one	navad-o yek	نود ویک
92 ninety-two	navad-o do	نود ودو
93 ninety-three	navad-o se	نود وسه

8. Cardinal numbers. Part 2

100 one hundred	sad	صد
200 two hundred	devist	دویست
300 three hundred	sisad	سیصد
400 four hundred	čāhārsad	چهارصد
500 five hundred	pānsad	پانصد

600 six hundred	šešsad	ششصد
700 seven hundred	haftsad	هفتصد
800 eight hundred	haštsad	هشتصد
900 nine hundred	nohsad	نهصد

1000 one thousand	hezār	هزار
2000 two thousand	dohezār	دوهزار
3000 three thousand	se hezār	سه هزار
10000 ten thousand	dah hezār	ده هزار
one hundred thousand	sad hezār	صد هزار
million	milyun	میلیون
billion	milyārd	میلیارد

9. Ordinal numbers

first (adj)	avvalin	اولین
second (adj)	dovvomin	دومین
third (adj)	sevvomin	سومین
fourth (adj)	čāhāromin	چهارمین

fifth (adj)	panjomin	پنجمین
sixth (adj)	šešomin	ششمین
seventh (adj)	haftomin	هفتمین
eighth (adj)	haštomin	هشتمین
ninth (adj)	nohomin	نهمین
tenth (adj)	dahomin	دهمین

COLOURS. UNITS OF MEASUREMENT

10. Colors

color	rang	رنگ
shade (tint)	teyf-e rang	طیف رنگ
hue	rangmaye	رنگمایه
rainbow	rangin kamān	رنگین کمان
white (adj)	sefid	سفید
black (adj)	siyāh	سیاه
gray (adj)	xākestari	خاکستری
green (adj)	sabz	سبز
yellow (adj)	zard	زرد
red (adj)	sorx	سرخ
blue (adj)	abi	آبی
light blue (adj)	ābi rowšan	آبی روشن
pink (adj)	surati	صورتی
orange (adj)	nārenji	نارنجی
violet (adj)	banafš	بنفش
brown (adj)	qahve i	قهوه ای
golden (adj)	talāyi	طلایی
silvery (adj)	noqre i	نقره ای
beige (adj)	baž	بژ
cream (adj)	kerem	کرم
turquoise (adj)	firuze i	فیروزه ای
cherry red (adj)	ālbāluyi	آلبالویی
lilac (adj)	banafš yasi	بنفش یاسی
crimson (adj)	zereški	زرشکی
light (adj)	rowšan	روشن
dark (adj)	tire	تیره
bright, vivid (adj)	rowšan	روشن
colored (pencils)	rangi	رنگی
color (e.g., ~ film)	rangi	رنگی
black-and-white (adj)	siyāh-o sefid	سیاه و سفید
plain (one-colored)	yek rang	یک رنگ
multicolored (adj)	rangārang	رنگارنگ

11. Units of measurement

weight	vazn	وزن
length	tul	طول
width	arz	عرض
height	ertefā'	ارتفاع
depth	omq	عمق
volume	hajm	حجم
area	masāhat	مساحت

gram	garm	گرم
milligram	mili geram	میلی گرم
kilogram	kilugeram	کیلوگرم
ton	ton	تن
pound	pond	پوند
ounce	ons	اونس

meter	metr	متر
millimeter	mili metr	میلی متر
centimeter	sāntimetr	سانتیمتر
kilometer	kilumetr	کیلومتر
mile	māyel	مایل

inch	inč	اینچ
foot	fowt	فوت
yard	yārd	یارد

| square meter | metr morabba' | متر مربع |
| hectare | hektār | هکتار |

liter	litr	لیتر
degree	daraje	درجه
volt	volt	ولت
ampere	āmper	آمپر
horsepower	asb-e boxār	اسب بخار

quantity	meqdār	مقدار
a little bit of ...	kami	کمی
half	nim	نیم

| dozen | dojin | دوجین |
| piece (item) | tā | تا |

| size | andāze | اندازه |
| scale (map ~) | meqyās | مقیاس |

minimal (adj)	haddeaqal	حداقل
the smallest (adj)	kučaktarin	کوچکترین
medium (adj)	motevasset	متوسط
maximal (adj)	haddeaksar	حداکثر
the largest (adj)	bištarin	بیشترین

12. Containers

canning jar (glass ~)	šišeh konserv	شیشه کنسرو
can	quti	قوطی
bucket	satl	سطل
barrel	boške	بشکه
wash basin (e.g., plastic ~)	tašt	تشت
tank (100L water ~)	maxzan	مخزن
hip flask	qomqome	قمقمه
jerrycan	dabbe	دبه
tank (e.g., tank car)	maxzan	مخزن
mug	livān	لیوان
cup (of coffee, etc.)	fenjān	فنجان
saucer	na'lbeki	نعلبکی
glass (tumbler)	estekān	استکان
wine glass	gilās-e šarāb	گیلاس شراب
stock pot (soup pot)	qāblame	قابلمه
bottle (~ of wine)	botri	بطری
neck (of the bottle, etc.)	gardan-e botri	گردن بطری
carafe (decanter)	tong	تنگ
pitcher	pārč	پارچ
vessel (container)	zarf	ظرف
pot (crock, stoneware ~)	sofāl	سفال
vase	goldān	گلدان
bottle (perfume ~)	botri	بطری
vial, small bottle	viyāl	ویال
tube (of toothpaste)	tiyub	تیوب
sack (bag)	kise	کیسه
bag (paper ~, plastic ~)	pākat	پاکت
pack (of cigarettes, etc.)	baste	بسته
box (e.g., shoebox)	ja'be	جعبه
crate	sanduq	صندوق
basket	sabad	سبد

MAIN VERBS

13. The most important verbs. Part 1

to advise (vt)	nasihat kardan	نصیحت کردن
to agree (say yes)	movāfeqat kardan	موافقت کردن
to answer (vi, vt)	javāb dādan	جواب دادن
to apologize (vi)	ozr xāstan	عذر خواستن
to arrive (vi)	residan	رسیدن
to ask (~ oneself)	porsidan	پرسیدن
to ask (~ sb to do sth)	xāstan	خواستن
to be (vi)	budan	بودن
to be afraid	tarsidan	ترسیدن
to be hungry	gorosne budan	گرسنه بودن
to be interested in ...	alāqe dāštan	علاقه داشتن
to be needed	hāmi budan	حامی بودن
to be surprised	mote'ajjeb šodan	متعجب شدن
to be thirsty	tešne budan	تشنه بودن
to begin (vt)	šoru' kardan	شروع کردن
to belong to ...	ta'alloq dāštan	تعلق داشتن
to boast (vi)	be rox kešidan	به رخ کشیدن
to break (split into pieces)	šekastan	شکستن
to call (~ for help)	komak xāstan	کمک خواستن
can (v aux)	tavānestan	توانستن
to catch (vt)	gereftan	گرفتن
to change (vt)	avaz kardan	عوض کردن
to choose (select)	entexāb kardan	انتخاب کردن
to come down (the stairs)	pāyin āmadan	پایین آمدن
to compare (vt)	moqāyse kardan	مقایسه کردن
to complain (vi, vt)	šekāyat kardan	شکایت کردن
to confuse (mix up)	qāti kardan	قاطی کردن
to continue (vt)	edāme dādan	ادامه دادن
to control (vt)	kontorol kardan	کنترل کردن
to cook (dinner)	poxtan	پختن
to cost (vt)	qeymat dāštan	قیمت داشتن
to count (add up)	šemordan	شمردن
to count on ...	hesāb kardan	حساب کردن
to create (vt)	ijād kardan	ایجاد کردن
to cry (weep)	gerye kardan	گریه کردن

14. The most important verbs. Part 2

to deceive (vi, vt)	farib dādan	فریب دادن
to decorate (tree, street)	tazyin kardan	تزیین کردن
to defend (a country, etc.)	defā' kardan	دفاع کردن
to demand (request firmly)	darxāst kardan	درخواست کردن
to dig (vt)	kandan	کندن
to discuss (vt)	bahs kardan	بحث کردن
to do (vt)	anjām dādan	انجام دادن
to doubt (have doubts)	šok dāštan	شک داشتن
to drop (let fall)	andāxtan	انداختن
to enter (room, house, etc.)	vāred šodan	وارد شدن
to excuse (forgive)	baxšidan	بخشیدن
to exist (vi)	vojud dāštan	وجود داشتن
to expect (foresee)	pišbini kardan	پیش بینی کردن
to explain (vt)	touzih dādan	توضیح دادن
to fall (vi)	oftādan	افتادن
to find (vt)	peydā kardan	پیدا کردن
to finish (vt)	be pāyān resāndan	به پایان رساندن
to fly (vi)	parvāz kardan	پرواز کردن
to follow ... (come after)	donbāl kardan	دنبال کردن
to forget (vi, vt)	farāmuš kardan	فراموش کردن
to forgive (vt)	baxšidan	بخشیدن
to give (vt)	dādan	دادن
to give a hint	sarnax dādan	سرنخ دادن
to go (on foot)	raftan	رفتن
to go for a swim	ābtani kardan	آبتنی کردن
to go out (for dinner, etc.)	birun raftan	بیرون رفتن
to guess (the answer)	hads zadan	حدس زدن
to have (vt)	dāštan	داشتن
to have breakfast	sobhāne xordan	صبحانه خوردن
to have dinner	šām xordan	شام خوردن
to have lunch	nāhār xordan	ناهار خوردن
to hear (vt)	šenidan	شنیدن
to help (vt)	komak kardan	کمک کردن
to hide (vt)	penhān kardan	پنهان کردن
to hope (vi, vt)	omid dāštan	امید داشتن
to hunt (vi, vt)	šekār kardan	شکار کردن
to hurry (vi)	ajale kardan	عجله کردن

15. The most important verbs. Part 3

to inform (vt)	āgah kardan	آگاه کردن
to insist (vi, vt)	esrār kardan	اصرار کردن
to insult (vt)	towhin kardan	توهین کردن
to invite (vt)	da'vat kardan	دعوت کردن
to joke (vi)	šuxi kardan	شوخی کردن
to keep (vt)	hefz kardan	حفظ کردن
to keep silent	sāket māndan	ساکت ماندن
to kill (vt)	koštan	کشتن
to know (sb)	šenāxtan	شناختن
to know (sth)	dānestan	دانستن
to laugh (vi)	xandidan	خندیدن
to liberate (city, etc.)	āzād kardan	آزاد کردن
to like (I like ...)	dust dāštan	دوست داشتن
to look for ... (search)	jostoju kardan	جستجو کردن
to love (sb)	dust dāštan	دوست داشتن
to make a mistake	eštebāh kardan	اشتباه کردن
to manage, to run	edāre kardan	اداره کردن
to mean (signify)	ma'ni dāštan	معنی داشتن
to mention (talk about)	zekr kardan	ذکر کردن
to miss (school, etc.)	qāyeb budan	غایب بودن
to notice (see)	motevajjeh šodan	متوجه شدن
to object (vi, vt)	moxalefat kardan	مخالفت کردن
to observe (see)	mošāhede kardan	مشاهده کردن
to open (vt)	bāz kardan	باز کردن
to order (meal, etc.)	sefāreš dādan	سفارش دادن
to order (mil.)	farmān dādan	فرمان دادن
to own (possess)	sāheb budan	صاحب بودن
to participate (vi)	šerekat kardan	شرکت کردن
to pay (vi, vt)	pardāxtan	پرداختن
to permit (vt)	ejāze dādan	اجازه دادن
to plan (vt)	barnāmerizi kardan	برنامه ریزی کردن
to play (children)	bāzi kardan	بازی کردن
to pray (vi, vt)	do'ā kardan	دعا کردن
to prefer (vt)	tarjih dādan	ترجیح دادن
to promise (vt)	qowl dādan	قول دادن
to pronounce (vt)	talaffoz kardan	تلفظ کردن
to propose (vt)	pišnahād dādan	پیشنهاد دادن
to punish (vt)	tanbih kardan	تنبیه کردن

16. The most important verbs. Part 4

to read (vi, vt)	xāndan	خواندن
to recommend (vt)	towsie kardan	توصیه کردن

to refuse (vi, vt)	rad kardan	رد کردن
to regret (be sorry)	afsus xordan	افسوس خوردن
to rent (sth from sb)	ejāre kardan	اجاره کردن

to repeat (say again)	tekrār kardan	تکرار کردن
to reserve, to book	rezerv kardan	رزرو کردن
to run (vi)	davidan	دویدن
to save (rescue)	najāt dādan	نجات دادن
to say (~ thank you)	goftan	گفتن

to scold (vt)	da'vā kardan	دعوا کردن
to see (vt)	didan	دیدن
to sell (vt)	foruxtan	فروختن
to send (vt)	ferestādan	فرستادن
to shoot (vi)	tirandāzi kardan	تیراندازی کردن

to shout (vi)	faryād zadan	فریاد زدن
to show (vt)	nešān dādan	نشان دادن
to sign (document)	emzā kardan	امضا کردن
to sit down (vi)	nešastan	نشستن

to smile (vi)	labxand zadan	لبخند زدن
to speak (vi, vt)	harf zadan	حرف زدن
to steal (money, etc.)	dozdidan	دزدیدن
to stop (for pause, etc.)	motevaghef šhodan	متوقف شدن
to stop (please ~ calling me)	bas kardan	بس کردن

to study (vt)	dars xāndan	درس خواندن
to swim (vi)	šenā kardan	شنا کردن
to take (vt)	bardāštan	برداشتن
to think (vi, vt)	fekr kardan	فکر کردن
to threaten (vt)	tahdid kardan	تهدید کردن

to touch (with hands)	lams kardan	لمس کردن
to translate (vt)	tarjome kardan	ترجمه کردن
to trust (vt)	etminān kardan	اطمینان کردن
to try (attempt)	talāš kardan	تلاش کردن
to turn (e.g., ~ left)	pičidan	پیچیدن

to underestimate (vt)	dast-e kam gereftan	دست کم گرفتن
to understand (vt)	fahmidan	فهمیدن
to unite (vt)	mottahed kardan	متحد کردن
to wait (vt)	montazer budan	منتظر بودن

to want (wish, desire)	xāstan	خواستن
to warn (vt)	hošdār dādan	هشدار دادن
to work (vi)	kār kardan	کار کردن
to write (vt)	neveštan	نوشتن
to write down	neveštan	نوشتن

TIME. CALENDAR

17. Weekdays

Monday	došanbe	دوشنبه
Tuesday	se šanbe	سه شنبه
Wednesday	čāhāršanbe	چهارشنبه
Thursday	panj šanbe	پنج شنبه
Friday	jomʻe	جمعه
Saturday	šanbe	شنبه
Sunday	yek šanbe	یک شنبه
today (adv)	emruz	امروز
tomorrow (adv)	fardā	فردا
the day after tomorrow	pas fardā	پس فردا
yesterday (adv)	diruz	دیروز
the day before yesterday	pariruz	پریروز
day	ruz	روز
working day	ruz-e kāri	روز کاری
public holiday	ruz-e jašn	روز جشن
day off	ruz-e taʻtil	روز تعطیل
weekend	āxar-e hafte	آخر هفته
all day long	tamām-e ruz	تمام روز
the next day (adv)	ruz-e baʻd	روز بعد
two days ago	do ruz-e piš	دو روز پیش
the day before	ruz-e qabl	روز قبل
daily (adj)	ruzāne	روزانه
every day (adv)	har ruz	هر روز
week	hafte	هفته
last week (adv)	hafte-ye gozašte	هفته گذشته
next week (adv)	hafte-ye āyande	هفته آینده
weekly (adj)	haftegi	هفتگی
every week (adv)	har hafte	هر هفته
twice a week	do bār dar hafte	دو بار درهفته
every Tuesday	har sešanbe	هر سه شنبه

18. Hours. Day and night

morning	sobh	صبح
in the morning	sobh	صبح
noon, midday	zohr	ظهر

in the afternoon	ba'd az zohr	بعد ازظهر
evening	asr	عصر
in the evening	asr	عصر
night	šab	شب
at night	šab	شب
midnight	nesfe šab	نصفه شب
second	sānie	ثانیه
minute	daqiqe	دقیقه
hour	sā'at	ساعت
half an hour	nim sā'at	نیم ساعت
a quarter-hour	yek rob'	یک ربع
fifteen minutes	pānzdah daqiqe	پانزده دقیقه
24 hours	šabāne ruz	شبانه روز
sunrise	tolu-'e āftāb	طلوع آفتاب
dawn	sahar	سحر
early morning	sobh-e zud	صبح زود
sunset	qorub	غروب
early in the morning	sobh-e zud	صبح زود
this morning	emruz sobh	امروز صبح
tomorrow morning	fardā sobh	فردا صبح
this afternoon	emruz zohr	امروز ظهر
in the afternoon	ba'd az zohr	بعد ازظهر
tomorrow afternoon	fardā ba'd az zohr	فردا بعد ازظهر
tonight (this evening)	emšab	امشب
tomorrow night	fardā šab	فردا شب
at 3 o'clock sharp	sar-e sā'at-e se	سر ساعت ۳
about 4 o'clock	nazdik-e sā'at-e čāhār	نزدیک ساعت ۴
by 12 o'clock	nazdik zohr	نزدیک ظهر
in 20 minutes	bist daqiqe-ye digar	۲۰ دقیقه دیگر
in an hour	yek sā'at-e digar	یک ساعت دیگر
on time (adv)	be moqe'	به موقع
a quarter of ...	yek rob' be	یک ربع به
within an hour	yek sā'at-e digar	یک ساعت دیگر
every 15 minutes	har pānzdah daqiqe	هر ۱۵ دقیقه
round the clock	šabāne ruz	شبانه روز

19. Months. Seasons

January	žānvie	ژانویه
February	fevriye	فوریه
March	mārs	مارس
April	āvril	آوریل

May	meh	مه
June	žuan	ژوئن
July	žuiye	ژوئیه
August	owt	اوت
September	septāmbr	سپتامبر
October	oktobr	اکتبر
November	novāmbr	نوامبر
December	desāmr	دسامبر
spring	bahār	بهار
in spring	dar bahār	در بهار
spring (as adj)	bahāri	بهاری
summer	tābestān	تابستان
in summer	dar tābestān	در تابستان
summer (as adj)	tābestāni	تابستانی
fall	pāyiz	پاییز
in fall	dar pāyiz	در پاییز
fall (as adj)	pāyizi	پاییزی
winter	zemestān	زمستان
in winter	dar zemestān	در زمستان
winter (as adj)	zemestāni	زمستانی
month	māh	ماه
this month	in māh	این ماه
next month	māh-e āyande	ماه آینده
last month	māh-e gozašte	ماه گذشته
a month ago	yek māh qabl	یک ماه قبل
in a month (a month later)	yek māh digar	یک ماه دیگر
in 2 months (2 months later)	do māh-e digar	۲ماه دیگر
the whole month	tamām-e māh	تمام ماه
all month long	tamām-e māh	تمام ماه
monthly (~ magazine)	māhāne	ماهانه
monthly (adv)	māhāne	ماهانه
every month	har māh	هر ماه
twice a month	do bār dar māh	دو بار درماه
year	sāl	سال
this year	emsāl	امسال
next year	sāl-e āyande	سال آینده
last year	sāl-e gozašte	سال گذشته
a year ago	yek sāl qabl	یک سال قبل
in a year	yek sāl-e digar	یک سال دیگر
in two years	do sāl-e digar	۲سال دیگر
the whole year	tamām-e sāl	تمام سال

all year long	tamām-e sāl	تمام سال
every year	har sāl	هر سال
annual (adj)	sālāne	سالانه
annually (adv)	sālāne	سالانه
4 times a year	čāhār bār dar sāl	چهار بار در سال
date (e.g., today's ~)	tārix	تاریخ
date (e.g., ~ of birth)	tārix	تاریخ
calendar	taqvim	تقویم
half a year	nim sāl	نیم سال
six months	nim sāl	نیم سال
season (summer, etc.)	fasl	فصل
century	qarn	قرن

TRAVEL. HOTEL

20. Trip. Travel

tourism, travel	gardešgari	گردشگری
tourist	turist	توریست
trip, voyage	mosāferat	مسافرت
adventure	mājarā	ماجرا
trip, journey	safar	سفر
vacation	moraxxasi	مرخصی
to be on vacation	dar moraxassi budan	در مرخصی بودن
rest	esterāhat	استراحت
train	qatār	قطار
by train	bā qatār	با قطار
airplane	havāpeymā	هواپیما
by airplane	bā havāpeymā	با هواپیما
by car	bā otomobil	با اتومبیل
by ship	dar kešti	با کشتی
luggage	bār	بار
suitcase	čamedān	چمدان
luggage cart	čarx-e hamle bar	چرخ حمل بار
passport	gozarnāme	گذرنامه
visa	ravādid	روادید
ticket	belit	بلیط
air ticket	belit-e havāpeymā	بلیط هواپیما
guidebook	ketāb-e rāhnamā	کتاب راهنما
map (tourist ~)	naqše	نقشه
area (rural ~)	mahal	محل
place, site	jā	جا
exotica (n)	qarāyeb	غرایب
exotic (adj)	qarib	غریب
amazing (adj)	heyrat angiz	حیرت انگیز
group	goruh	گروه
excursion, sightseeing tour	gardeš	گردش
guide (person)	rāhnamā-ye tur	راهنمای تور

21. Hotel

hotel	hotel	هتل
motel	motel	متل
three-star (~ hotel)	se setāre	سه ستاره
five-star	panj setāre	پنج ستاره
to stay (in a hotel, etc.)	māndan	ماندن
room	otāq	اتاق
single room	otāq-e yeknafare	اتاق یک نفره
double room	otāq-e do nafare	اتاق دو نفره
to book a room	otāq rezerv kardan	اتاق رزرو کردن
half board	nim pānsiyon	نیم پانسیون
full board	pānsiyon	پانسیون
with bath	bā vān	با وان
with shower	bā duš	با دوش
satellite television	televiziyon-e māhvārei	تلویزیون ماهواره ای
air-conditioner	tahviye-ye matbu'	تهویه مطبوع
towel	howle	حوله
key	kelid	کلید
administrator	edāre-ye konande	اداره کننده
chambermaid	mostaxdem	مستخدم
porter, bellboy	bārbar	باربر
doorman	darbān	دربان
restaurant	resturān	رستوران
pub, bar	bār	بار
breakfast	sobhāne	صبحانه
dinner	šām	شام
buffet	bufe	بوفه
lobby	lābi	لابی
elevator	āsānsor	آسانسور
DO NOT DISTURB	mozāhem našavid	مزاحم نشوید
NO SMOKING	sigār kešidan mamnu'	سیگار کشیدن ممنوع

22. Sightseeing

monument	mojassame	مجسمه
fortress	qal'e	قلعه
palace	kāx	کاخ
castle	qal'e	قلعه
tower	borj	برج
mausoleum	ārāmgāh	آرامگاه

architecture	me'māri	معماری
medieval (adj)	qorun-e vasati	قرون وسطی
ancient (adj)	qadimi	قدیمی
national (adj)	melli	ملی
famous (monument, etc.)	mašhur	مشهور

tourist	turist	توریست
guide (person)	rāhnamā-ye tur	راهنمای تور
excursion, sightseeing tour	gardeš	گردش
to show (vt)	nešān dādan	نشان دادن
to tell (vt)	hekāyat kardan	حکایت کردن

to find (vt)	peydā kardan	پیدا کردن
to get lost (lose one's way)	gom šodan	گم شدن
map (e.g., subway ~)	naqše	نقشه
map (e.g., city ~)	naqše	نقشه

souvenir, gift	sowqāti	سوغاتی
gift shop	forušgāh-e sowqāti	فروشگاه سوغاتی
to take pictures	aks gereftan	عکس گرفتن
to have one's picture taken	aks gereftan	عکس گرفتن

TRANSPORTATION

23. Airport

airport	forudgāh	فرودگاه
airplane	havāpeymā	هواپیما
airline	šerkat-e havāpeymāyi	شرکت هواپیمایی
air traffic controller	ma'mur-e kontorol-e terāfik-e havāyi	مأمور کنترل ترافیک هوایی
departure	azimat	عزیمت
arrival	vorud	ورود
to arrive (by plane)	residan	رسیدن
departure time	zamān-e parvāz	زمان پرواز
arrival time	zamān-e vorud	زمان ورود
to be delayed	ta'xir kardan	تأخیر کردن
flight delay	ta'xir-e parvāz	تأخیر پرواز
information board	tāblo-ye ettelā'āt	تابلوی اطلاعات
information	ettelā'āt	اطلاعات
to announce (vt)	e'lām kardan	اعلام کردن
flight (e.g., next ~)	parvāz	پرواز
customs	gomrok	گمرک
customs officer	ma'mur-e gomrok	مأمور گمرک
customs declaration	ežhār-nāme	اظهارنامه
to fill out (vt)	por kardan	پر کردن
to fill out the declaration	ežhār-nāme rā por kardan	اظهارنامه را پر کردن
passport control	kontorol-e gozarnāme	کنترل گذرنامه
luggage	bār	بار
hand luggage	bār-e dasti	بار دستی
luggage cart	čarx-e hamle bar	چرخ حمل بار
landing	forud	فرود
landing strip	bānd-e forudgāh	باند فرودگاه
to land (vi)	nešastan	نشستن
airstairs	pellekān	پلکان
check-in	ček in	چک این
check-in counter	bāje-ye kontorol	باجه کنترل
to check-in (vi)	čekin kardan	چکاین کردن
boarding pass	kārt-e parvāz	کارت پرواز

departure gate	gi-yat xoruj	گیت خروج
transit	terānzit	ترانزیت
to wait (vt)	montazer budan	منتظر بودن
departure lounge	tālār-e entezār	تالار انتظار
to see off	badraqe kardan	بدرقه کردن
to say goodbye	xodāhāfezi kardan	خداحافظی کردن

24. Airplane

airplane	havāpeymā	هواپیما
air ticket	belit-e havāpeymā	بلیط هواپیما
airline	šerkat-e havāpeymāyi	شرکت هواپیمایی
airport	forudgāh	فرودگاه
supersonic (adj)	māvarā sowt	ماوراء صوت

captain	kāpitān	کاپیتان
crew	xadame	خدمه
pilot	xalabān	خلبان
flight attendant (fem.)	mehmāndār-e havāpeymā	مهماندار هواپیما
navigator	nāvbar	ناویر

wings	bāl-hā	بال ها
tail	dam	دم
cockpit	kābin	کابین
engine	motor	موتور
undercarriage (landing gear)	šāssi	شاسی
turbine	turbin	توربین

propeller	parvāne	پروانه
black box	ja'be-ye siyāh	جعبه سیاه
yoke (control column)	farmān	فرمان
fuel	suxt	سوخت

safety card	dasturol'amal	دستورالعمل
oxygen mask	māsk-e oksižen	ماسک اکسیژن
uniform	oniform	اونیفورم
life vest	jeliqe-ye nejāt	جلیقه نجات
parachute	čatr-e nejāt	چترنجات

takeoff	parvāz	پرواز
to take off (vi)	parvāz kardan	پرواز کردن
runway	bānd-e forudgāh	باند فرودگاه

visibility	meydān did	میدان دید
flight (act of flying)	parvāz	پرواز
altitude	ertefā'	ارتفاع
air pocket	čāle-ye havāyi	چاله هوایی
seat	jā	جا
headphones	guši	گوشی

folding tray (tray table)	sini-ye tāšow	سینی تاشو
airplane window	panjere	پنجره
aisle	rāhrow	راهرو

25. Train

train	qatār	قطار
commuter train	qatār-e barqi	قطار برقی
express train	qatār-e sari'osseyr	قطارسریع السیر
diesel locomotive	lokomotiv-e dizel	لوکوموتیو دیزل
steam locomotive	lokomotiv-e boxar	لوکوموتیو بخار

| passenger car | vāgon | واگن |
| dining car | vāgon-e resturān | واگن رستوران |

rails	reyl-hā	ریل ها
railroad	rāh āhan	راه آهن
railway tie	reyl-e band	ریل بند

platform (railway ~)	sakku-ye rāh-āhan	سکوی راه آهن
track (~ 1, 2, etc.)	masir	مسیر
semaphore	nešanar	نشانبر
station	istgāh	ایستگاه

engineer (train driver)	rānande	راننده
porter (of luggage)	bārbar	باربر
car attendant	rāhnamā-ye qatār	راهنمای قطار
passenger	mosāfer	مسافر
conductor (ticket inspector)	kontorol či	کنترل چی

| corridor (in train) | rāhrow | راهرو |
| emergency brake | tormoz-e ezterāri | ترمز اضطراری |

compartment	kupe	کوپه
berth	taxt-e kupe	تخت کوپه
upper berth	taxt-e bālā	تخت بالا
lower berth	taxt-e pāyin	تخت پایین
bed linen, bedding	raxt-e xāb	رخت خواب

ticket	belit	بلیط
schedule	barnāme	برنامه
information display	barnāme-ye zamāni	برنامه زمانی

to leave, to depart	tark kardan	ترک کردن
departure (of train)	harekat	حرکت
to arrive (ab. train)	residan	رسیدن
arrival	vorud	ورود
to arrive by train	bā qatār āmadan	با قطار آمدن
to get on the train	savār-e qatār šodan	سوار قطار شدن

to get off the train	az qatār piyāde šodan	از قطار پیاده شدن
train wreck	sānehe	سانحه
to derail (vi)	az xat xārej šodan	از خط خارج شدن

steam locomotive	lokomotiv-e boxar	لوکوموتیو بخار
stoker, fireman	ātaškār	آتشکار
firebox	ātašdān	آتشدان
coal	zoqāl sang	زغال سنگ

26. Ship

| ship | kešti | کشتی |
| vessel | kešti | کشتی |

steamship	kešti-ye boxāri	کشتی بخاری
riverboat	qāyeq-e rudxāne	قایق رودخانه
cruise ship	kešti-ye tafrihi	کشتی تفریحی
cruiser	razm nāv	رزم ناو

yacht	qāyeq-e tafrihi	قایق تفریحی
tugboat	yadak keš	یدک کش
barge	kešti-ye bārkeše yadaki	کشتی بارکش یدکی
ferry	kešti-ye farābar	کشتی فرابر

| sailing ship | kešti-ye bādbāni | کشتی بادبانی |
| brigantine | košti dozdān daryā-yi | کشتی دزدان دریایی |

| ice breaker | kešti-ye yaxšekan | کشتی یخ شکن |
| submarine | zirdaryāyi | زیردریایی |

boat (flat-bottomed ~)	qāyeq	قایق
dinghy	qāyeq-e tafrihi	قایق تفریحی
lifeboat	qāyeq-e nejāt	قایق نجات
motorboat	qāyeq-e motori	قایق موتوری

captain	kāpitān	کاپیتان
seaman	malavān	ملوان
sailor	malavān	ملوان
crew	xadame	خدمه

boatswain	sar malavān	سر ملوان
ship's boy	šāgerd-e malavān	شاگرد ملوان
cook	āšpaz-e kešti	آشپز کشتی
ship's doctor	pezešk-e kešti	پزشک کشتی

deck	arše-ye kešti	عرشهٔ کشتی
mast	dakal	دکل
sail	bādbān	بادبان
hold	anbār	انبار
bow (prow)	sine-ye kešti	سینه کشتی

stern	aqab kešti	عقب کشتی
oar	pāru	پارو
screw propeller	parvāne	پروانه

cabin	otāq-e kešti	اتاق کشتی
wardroom	otāq-e afsarān	اتاق افسران
engine room	motor xāne	موتور خانه
bridge	pol-e farmāndehi	پل فرماندهی
radio room	kābin-e bisim	کابین بی سیم
wave (radio)	mowj	موج
logbook	roxdād nāme	رخداد نامه

spyglass	teleskop	تلسکوپ
bell	nāqus	ناقوس
flag	parčam	پرچم

| hawser (mooring ~) | tanāb | طناب |
| knot (bowline, etc.) | gereh | گره |

| deckrails | narde | نرده |
| gangway | pol | پل |

anchor	langar	لنگر
to weigh anchor	langar kešidan	لنگر کشیدن
to drop anchor	langar andāxtan	لنگر انداختن
anchor chain	zanjir-e langar	زنجیر لنگر

port (harbor)	bandar	بندر
quay, wharf	eskele	اسکله
to berth (moor)	pahlu gereftan	پهلو گرفتن
to cast off	tark kardan	ترک کردن

trip, voyage	mosāferat	مسافرت
cruise (sea trip)	safar-e daryāyi	سفر دریایی
course (route)	masir	مسیر
route (itinerary)	masir	مسیر

fairway (safe water channel)	kešti-ye ru	کشتی رو
shallows	mahall-e kam omq	محل کم عمق
to run aground	be gel nešastan	به گل نشستن

storm	tufān	طوفان
signal	alāmat	علامت
to sink (vi)	qarq šodan	غرق شدن
Man overboard!	kas-i dar hāl-e qarq šodan-ast!	کسی در حال غرق شدن است!

| SOS (distress signal) | sos | SOS |
| ring buoy | kamarband-e nejāt | کمربند نجات |

CITY

27. Urban transportation

bus	otobus	اتوبوس
streetcar	terāmvā	تراموا
trolley bus	otobus-e barqi	اتوبوس برقی
route (of bus, etc.)	xat	خط
number (e.g., bus ~)	šomāre	شماره
to go by ...	raftan bā	رفتن با
to get on (~ the bus)	savār šodan	سوار شدن
to get off ...	piyāde šodan	پیاده شدن
stop (e.g., bus ~)	istgāh-e otobus	ایستگاه اتوبوس
next stop	istgāh-e ba'di	ایستگاه بعدی
terminus	istgāh-e āxar	ایستگاه آخر
schedule	barnāme	برنامه
to wait (vt)	montazer budan	منتظر بودن
ticket	belit	بلیط
fare	qeymat-e belit	قیمت بلیط
cashier (ticket seller)	sanduqdār	صندوقدار
ticket inspection	kontorol-e belit	کنترل بلیط
ticket inspector	kontorol či	کنترل چی
to be late (for ...)	ta'xir dāštan	تأخیرداشتن
to miss (~ the train, etc.)	az dast dādan	از دست دادن
to be in a hurry	ajale kardan	عجله کردن
taxi, cab	tāksi	تاکسی
taxi driver	rānande-ye tāksi	راننده تاکسی
by taxi	bā tāksi	با تاکسی
taxi stand	istgāh-e tāksi	ایستگاه تاکسی
to call a taxi	tāksi gereftan	تاکسی گرفتن
to take a taxi	tāksi gereftan	تاکسی گرفتن
traffic	obur-o morur	عبور و مرور
traffic jam	terāfik	ترافیک
rush hour	sā'at-e šoluqi	ساعت شلوغی
to park (vi)	pārk kardan	پارک کردن
to park (vt)	pārk kardan	پارک کردن
parking lot	pārking	پارکینگ
subway	metro	مترو
station	istgāh	ایستگاه

to take the subway	bā metro raftan	با مترو رفتن
train	qatār	قطار
train station	istgāh-e rāh-e āhan	ایستگاه راه آهن

28. City. Life in the city

city, town	šahr	شهر
capital city	pāytaxt	پایتخت
village	rustā	روستا

city map	naqše-ye šahr	نقشهٔ شهر
downtown	markaz-e šahr	مرکز شهر
suburb	hume-ye šahr	حومهٔ شهر
suburban (adj)	hume-ye šahr	حومهٔ شهر

outskirts	hume	حومه
environs (suburbs)	hume	حومه
city block	mahalle	محله
residential block (area)	mahalle-ye maskuni	محلهٔ مسکونی

traffic	obur-o morur	عبور و مرور
traffic lights	čerāq-e rāhnamā	چراغ راهنما
public transportation	haml-o naql-e šahri	حمل و نقل شهری
intersection	čahārrāh	چهارراه

crosswalk	xatt-e āber-e piyāde	خط عابرپیاده
pedestrian underpass	zir-e gozar	زیر گذر
to cross (~ the street)	obur kardan	عبور کردن
pedestrian	piyāde	پیاده
sidewalk	piyāde row	پیاده رو

bridge	pol	پل
embankment (river walk)	xiyābān-e sāheli	خیابان ساحلی
fountain	češme	چشمه

allée (garden walkway)	bāq rāh	باغ راه
park	pārk	پارک
boulevard	bolvār	بولوار
square	meydān	میدان
avenue (wide street)	xiyābān	خیابان
street	xiyābān	خیابان
side street	kuče	کوچه
dead end	bon bast	بن بست

house	xāne	خانه
building	sāxtemān	ساختمان
skyscraper	āsemānxarāš	آسمانخراش

| facade | namā | نما |
| roof | bām | بام |

window	panjere	پنجره
arch	tāq-e qowsi	طاق قوسی
column	sotun	ستون
corner	nabš	نبش

store window	vitrin	ویترین
signboard (store sign, etc.)	tāblo	تابلو
poster	poster	پوستر
advertising poster	poster-e tabliqāti	پوستر تبلیغاتی
billboard	bilbord	بیلبورد

garbage, trash	āšqāl	آشغال
trashcan (public ~)	satl-e āšqāl	سطل آشغال
to litter (vi)	kasif kardan	کثیف کردن
garbage dump	jā-ye dafn-e āšqāl	جای دفن آشغال

phone booth	kābin-e telefon	کابین تلفن
lamppost	tir-e barq	تیر برق
bench (park ~)	nimkat	نیمکت

police officer	polis	پلیس
police	polis	پلیس
beggar	gedā	گدا
homeless (n)	bi xānomān	بی خانمان

29. Urban institutions

store	maqāze	مغازه
drugstore, pharmacy	dāruxāne	داروخانه
eyeglass store	eynak foruši	عینک فروشی
shopping mall	markaz-e tejāri	مرکز تجاری
supermarket	supermārket	سوپرمارکت

bakery	nānvāyi	نانوایی
baker	nānvā	نانوا
pastry shop	qannādi	قنادی
grocery store	baqqāli	بقالی
butcher shop	gušt foruši	گوشت فروشی

| produce store | sabzi foruši | سبزی فروشی |
| market | bāzār | بازار |

coffee house	kāfe	کافه
restaurant	resturān	رستوران
pub, bar	bār	بار
pizzeria	pitzā-foruši	پیتزا فروشی

hair salon	ārāyešgāh	آرایشگاه
post office	post	پست
dry cleaners	xošk-šuyi	خشک‌شویی

photo studio	ātolye-ye akkāsi	آتلیهٔ عکاسی
shoe store	kafš foruši	کفش فروشی
bookstore	ketāb-foruši	کتاب فروشی
sporting goods store	maqāze-ye varzeši	مغازهٔ ورزشی

clothes repair shop	ta'mir-e lebās	تعمیر لباس
formal wear rental	kerāye-ye lebās	کرایة لباس
video rental store	kerāye-ye film	کرایة فیلم

circus	sirak	سیرک
zoo	bāq-e vahš	باغ وحش
movie theater	sinamā	سینما
museum	muze	موزه
library	ketābxāne	کتابخانه

theater	teātr	تئاتر
opera (opera house)	operā	اپرا
nightclub	kābāre	کاباره
casino	kāzino	کازینو

mosque	masjed	مسجد
synagogue	kenešt	کنشت
cathedral	kelisā-ye jāme'	کلیسای جامع
temple	ma'bad	معبد
church	kelisā	کلیسا

college	anistito	انستیتو
university	dānešgāh	دانشگاه
school	madrese	مدرسه

prefecture	ostāndāri	استانداری
city hall	šahrdāri	شهرداری
hotel	hotel	هتل
bank	bānk	بانک

embassy	sefārat	سفارت
travel agency	āžāns-e jahāngardi	آژانس جهانگردی
information office	daftar-e ettelāāt	دفتر اطلاعات
currency exchange	sarrāfi	صرافی

| subway | metro | مترو |
| hospital | bimārestān | بیمارستان |

| gas station | pomp-e benzin | پمپ بنزین |
| parking lot | pārking | پارکینگ |

30. Signs

| signboard (store sign, etc.) | tāblo | تابلو |
| notice (door sign, etc.) | nevešte | نوشته |

poster	poster	پوستر
direction sign	rāhnamā	راهنما
arrow (sign)	alāmat	علامت

caution	ehtiyāt	احتیاط
warning sign	alāmat-e hošdār	علامت هشدار
to warn (vt)	hošdār dādan	هشدار دادن

rest day (weekly ~)	ruz-e ta'til	روز تعطیل
timetable (schedule)	jadval	جدول
opening hours	sā'athā-ye kāri	ساعت های کاری

WELCOME!	xoš āmadid	خوش آمدید
ENTRANCE	vorud	ورود
EXIT	xoruj	خروج

PUSH	hel dādan	هل دادن
PULL	bekešid	بکشید
OPEN	bāz	باز
CLOSED	baste	بسته

WOMEN	zanāne	زنانه
MEN	mardāne	مردانه

DISCOUNTS	taxfif	تخفیف
SALE	harāj	حراج

NEW!	jadid	جدید
FREE	majjāni	مجانی

ATTENTION!	tavajjoh	توجه
NO VACANCIES	otāq-e xāli nadārim	اتاق خالی نداریم
RESERVED	rezerv šode	رزرو شده

ADMINISTRATION	edāre	اداره
STAFF ONLY	xāse personel	خاص پرسنل

BEWARE OF THE DOG!	movāzeb-e sag bāšid	مواظب سگ باشید
NO SMOKING	sigār kešidan mamnu'	سیگار کشیدن ممنوع
DO NOT TOUCH!	dast nazanid	دست نزنید

DANGEROUS	xatarnāk	خطرناک
DANGER	xatar	خطر
HIGH VOLTAGE	voltāj bālā	ولتاژ بالا

NO SWIMMING!	šenā mamnu'	شنا ممنوع
OUT OF ORDER	xārāb	خراب

FLAMMABLE	qābel-e ehterāq	قابل احتراق
FORBIDDEN	mamnu'	ممنوع
NO TRESPASSING!	obur mamnu'	عبور ممنوع
WET PAINT	rang-e xis	رنگ خیس

31. Shopping

to buy (purchase)	xarid kardan	خرید کردن
purchase	xarid	خرید
to go shopping	xarid kardan	خرید کردن
shopping	xarid	خرید
to be open (ab. store)	bāz budan	باز بودن
to be closed	baste budan	بسته بودن
footwear, shoes	kafš	کفش
clothes, clothing	lebās	لباس
cosmetics	lavāzem-e ārāyeši	لوازم آرایشی
food products	mavādd-e qazāyi	مواد غذایی
gift, present	hedye	هدیه
salesman	forušande	فروشنده
saleswoman	forušande-ye zan	فروشنده زن
check out, cash desk	sanduq	صندوق
mirror	āyene	آینه
counter (store ~)	pišxān	پیشخوان
fitting room	otāq porov	اتاق پرو
to try on	emtehān kardan	امتحان کردن
to fit (ab. dress, etc.)	monāseb budan	مناسب بودن
to like (I like ...)	dust dāštan	دوست داشتن
price	qeymat	قیمت
price tag	barčasb-e qeymat	برچسب قیمت
to cost (vt)	qeymat dāštan	قیمت داشتن
How much?	čeqadr?	چقدر؟
discount	taxfif	تخفیف
inexpensive (adj)	arzān	ارزان
cheap (adj)	arzān	ارزان
expensive (adj)	gerān	گران
It's expensive	gerān ast	گران است
rental (n)	kerāye	کرایه
to rent (~ a tuxedo)	kerāye kardan	کرایه کردن
credit (trade credit)	vām	وام
on credit (adv)	xarid-e e'tebāri	خرید اعتباری

CLOTHING & ACCESSORIES

32. Outerwear. Coats

clothes	lebās	لباس
outerwear	lebās-e ru	لباس رو
winter clothing	lebās-e zemestāni	لباس زمستانی
coat (overcoat)	pāltow	پالتو
fur coat	pālto-ye pustin	پالتوی پوستین
fur jacket	kot-e pustin	کت پوستین
down coat	kāpšan	کاپشن
jacket (e.g., leather ~)	kot	کت
raincoat (trenchcoat, etc.)	bārāni	بارانی
waterproof (adj)	zed-e āb	ضد آب

33. Men's & women's clothing

shirt (button shirt)	pirāhan	پیراهن
pants	šalvār	شلوار
jeans	jin	جین
suit jacket	kot	کت
suit	kat-o šalvār	کت و شلوار
dress (frock)	lebās	لباس
skirt	dāman	دامن
blouse	boluz	بلوز
knitted jacket (cardigan, etc.)	jeliqe-ye kešbāf	جلیقه کشباف
jacket (of woman's suit)	kot	کت
T-shirt	tey šarr-at	تی شرت
shorts (short trousers)	šalvarak	شلوارک
tracksuit	lebās-e varzeši	لباس ورزشی
bathrobe	howle-ye hamām	حوله حمام
pajamas	pižāme	پیژامه
sweater	poliver	پلیور
pullover	poliver	پلیور
vest	jeliqe	جلیقه
tailcoat	kat-e dāman gerd	کت دامن گرد
tuxedo	esmoking	اسموکینگ

uniform	oniform	اونیفورم
workwear	lebās-e kār	لباس کار
overalls	rupuš	روپوش
coat (e.g., doctor's smock)	rupuš	روپوش

34. Clothing. Underwear

underwear	lebās-e zir	لباس زیر
boxers, briefs	šort-e bākser	شورت باکسر
panties	šort-e zanāne	شورت زنانه
undershirt (A-shirt)	zir-e pirāhan-i	زیر پیراهنی
socks	jurāb	جوراب

nightgown	lebās-e xāb	لباس خواب
bra	sine-ye band	سینه بند
knee highs (knee-high socks)	sāq	ساق
pantyhose	jurāb-e šalvāri	جوراب شلواری
stockings (thigh highs)	jurāb-e sāqeboland	جوراب ساقه بلند
bathing suit	māyo	مایو

35. Headwear

hat	kolāh	کلاه
fedora	šāpo	شاپو
baseball cap	kolāh beysbāl	کلاه بیس بال
flatcap	kolāh-e taxt	کلاه تخت

beret	kolāh barre	کلاه بره
hood	kolāh-e bārāni	کلاه بارانی
panama hat	kolāh-e dowre-ye boland	کلاه دوره بلند
knit cap (knitted hat)	kolāh-e bāftani	کلاه بافتنی

headscarf	rusari	روسری
women's hat	kolāh-e zanāne	کلاه زنانه
hard hat	kolāh-e imeni	کلاه ایمنی
garrison cap	kolāh-e pādegān	کلاه پادگان
helmet	kolāh-e imeni	کلاه ایمنی

| derby | kolāh-e namadi | کلاه نمدی |
| top hat | kolāh-e ostovānei | کلاه استوانه ای |

36. Footwear

| footwear | kafš | کفش |
| shoes (men's shoes) | putin | پوتین |

shoes (women's shoes)	kafš	كفش
boots (e.g., cowboy ~)	čakme	چکمه
slippers	dampāyi	دمپایی

tennis shoes (e.g., Nike ~)	kafš katān-i	كفش كتانی
sneakers	kafš katān-i	كفش كتانی
(e.g., Converse ~)		
sandals	sandal	صندل

cobbler (shoe repairer)	kaffāš	كفاش
heel	pāšne-ye kafš	پاشنهٔ كفش
pair (of shoes)	yek joft	یک جفت

shoestring	band-e kafš	بند كفش
to lace (vt)	band-e kafš bastan	بند كفش بستن
shoehorn	pāšne keš	پاشنه كش
shoe polish	vāks	واكس

37. Personal accessories

gloves	dastkeš	دستكش
mittens	dastkeš-e yek angošti	دستكش یک انگشتی
scarf (muffler)	šāl-e gardan	شال گردن

glasses (eyeglasses)	eynak	عینک
frame (eyeglass ~)	qāb	قاب
umbrella	čatr	چتر
walking stick	asā	عصا

| hairbrush | bores-e mu | برس مو |
| fan | bādbezan | بادبزن |

| tie (necktie) | kerāvāt | كراوات |
| bow tie | pāpiyon | پاپیون |

| suspenders | band šalvār | بند شلوار |
| handkerchief | dastmāl | دستمال |

| comb | šāne | شانه |
| barrette | sanjāq-e mu | سنجاق مو |

| hairpin | sanjāq-e mu | سنجاق مو |
| buckle | sagak | سگک |

| belt | kamarband | كمربند |
| shoulder strap | tasme | تسمه |

bag (handbag)	keyf	كیف
purse	keyf-e zanāne	كیف زنانه
backpack	kule pošti	كوله پشتی

38. Clothing. Miscellaneous

fashion	mod	مد
in vogue (adj)	mod	مد
fashion designer	tarrāh-e lebas	طراح لباس
collar	yaqe	یقه
pocket	jib	جیب
pocket (as adj)	jibi	جیبی
sleeve	āstin	آستین
hanging loop	band-e āviz	بند آویز
fly (on trousers)	zip	زیپ
zipper (fastener)	zip	زیپ
fastener	sagak	سگک
button	dokme	دکمه
buttonhole	surāx-e dokme	سوراخ دکمه
to come off (ab. button)	kande šodan	کنده شدن
to sew (vi, vt)	duxtan	دوختن
to embroider (vi, vt)	golduzi kardan	گلدوزی کردن
embroidery	golduzi	گلدوزی
sewing needle	suzan	سوزن
thread	nax	نخ
seam	darz	درز
to get dirty (vi)	kasif šodan	کثیف شدن
stain (mark, spot)	lakke	لکه
to crease, crumple (vi)	čoruk šodan	چروک شدن
to tear, to rip (vt)	pāre kardan	پاره کردن
clothes moth	šab parre	شب پره

39. Personal care. Cosmetics

toothpaste	xamir-e dandān	خمیر دندان
toothbrush	mesvāk	مسواک
to brush one's teeth	mesvāk zadan	مسواک زدن
razor	tiq	تیغ
shaving cream	kerem-e riš tarāši	کرم ریش تراشی
to shave (vi)	riš tarāšidan	ریش تراشیدن
soap	sābun	صابون
shampoo	šāmpu	شامپو
scissors	qeyči	قیچی
nail file	sohan-e nāxon	سوهان ناخن
nail clippers	nāxon gir	ناخن گیر
tweezers	mučin	موچین

cosmetics	lavāzem-e ārāyeši	لوازم آرایشی
face mask	māsk	ماسک
manicure	mānikur	مانیکور
to have a manicure	mānikur kardan	مانیکور کردن
pedicure	pedikur	پدیکور

make-up bag	kife lavāzem-e ārāyeši	کیف لوازم آرایشی
face powder	pudr	پودر
powder compact	ja'be-ye pudr	جعبهٔ پودر
blusher	sorxāb	سرخاب

perfume (bottled)	atr	عطر
toilet water (lotion)	atr	عطر
lotion	losiyon	لوسیون
cologne	odkolon	اودکلن

eyeshadow	sāye-ye češm	سایه چشم
eyeliner	medād čašm	مداد چشم
mascara	rimel	ریمل

lipstick	mātik	ماتیک
nail polish, enamel	lāk-e nāxon	لاک ناخن
hair spray	esperey-ye mu	اسپری مو
deodorant	deodyrant	دئودورانت

cream	kerem	کرم
face cream	kerem-e surat	کرم صورت
hand cream	kerem-e dast	کرم دست
anti-wrinkle cream	kerem-e zedd-e čoruk	کرم ضد چروک
day cream	kerem-e ruz	کرم روز
night cream	kerem-e šab	کرم شب
day (as adj)	ruzāne	روزانه
night (as adj)	šab	شب

tampon	tāmpon	تامپون
toilet paper (toilet roll)	kāqaz-e tuālet	کاغذ توالت
hair dryer	sešovār	سشوار

40. Watches. Clocks

watch (wristwatch)	sā'at-e mochi	ساعت مچی
dial	safhe-ye sā'at	صفحهٔ ساعت
hand (of clock, watch)	aqrabe	عقربه
metal watch band	band-e sāat	بند ساعت
watch strap	band-e čarmi	بند چرمی

battery	bātri	باطری
to be dead (battery)	tamām šodan bātri	تمام شدن باتری
to change a battery	bātri avaz kardan	باطری عوض کردن
to run fast	jelo oftādan	جلو افتادن

to run slow	aqab māndan	عقب ماندن
wall clock	sā'at-e divāri	ساعت دیواری
hourglass	sā'at-e šeni	ساعت شنی
sundial	sā'at-e āftābi	ساعت آفتابی
alarm clock	sā'at-e zang dār	ساعت زنگ دار
watchmaker	sā'at sāz	ساعت ساز
to repair (vt)	ta'mir kardan	تعمیر کردن

EVERYDAY EXPERIENCE

41. Money

money	pul	پول
currency exchange	tabdil-e arz	تبدیل ارز
exchange rate	nerx-e arz	نرخ ارز
ATM	xodpardāz	خودپرداز
coin	sekke	سکه

dollar	dolār	دلار
euro	yuro	یورو

lira	lire	لیره
Deutschmark	mārk	مارک
franc	farānak	فرانک
pound sterling	pond-e esterling	پوند استرلینگ
yen	yen	ین

debt	qarz	قرض
debtor	bedehkār	بدهکار
to lend (money)	qarz dādan	قرض دادن
to borrow (vi, vt)	qarz gereftan	قرض گرفتن

bank	bānk	بانک
account	hesāb-e bānki	حساب بانکی
to deposit (vt)	rixtan	ریختن
to deposit into the account	be hesāb rixtan	به حساب ریختن
to withdraw (vt)	az hesāb bardāštan	از حساب برداشتن

credit card	kārt-e e'tebāri	کارت اعتباری
cash	pul-e naqd	پول نقد
check	ček	چک
to write a check	ček neveštan	چک نوشتن
checkbook	daste-ye ček	دسته چک

wallet	kif-e pul	کیف پول
change purse	kif-e pul	کیف پول
safe	gāvsanduq	گاوصندوق

heir	vāres	وارث
inheritance	mirās	میراث
fortune (wealth)	dārāyi	دارایی

lease	ejāre	اجاره
rent (money)	kerāye-ye xāne	کرایۀ خانه

to rent (sth from sb)	ejāre kardan	اجاره کردن
price	qeymat	قیمت
cost	arzeš	ارزش
sum	jam'-e kol	جمع کل

to spend (vt)	xarj kardan	خرج کردن
expenses	maxārej	مخارج
to economize (vi, vt)	sarfeju-yi kardan	صرفه جویی کردن
economical	maqrun besarfe	مقرون به صرفه

to pay (vi, vt)	pardāxtan	پرداختن
payment	pardāxt	پرداخت
change (give the ~)	pul-e xerad	پول خرد

tax	māliyāt	مالیات
fine	jarime	جریمه
to fine (vt)	jarime kardan	جریمه کردن

42. Post. Postal service

post office	post	پست
mail (letters, etc.)	post	پست
mailman	nāme resān	نامه رسان
opening hours	sā'athā-ye kāri	ساعت های کاری

letter	nāme	نامه
registered letter	nāme-ye sefāreši	نامه سفارشی
postcard	kārt-e postāl	کارت پستال
telegram	telegrām	تلگرام
package (parcel)	baste posti	بسته پستی
money transfer	havāle	حواله

to receive (vt)	gereftan	گرفتن
to send (vt)	ferestādan	فرستادن
sending	ersāl	ارسال

address	nešāni	نشانی
ZIP code	kod-e posti	کد پستی
sender	ferestande	فرستنده
receiver	girande	گیرنده

name (first name)	esm	اسم
surname (last name)	nām-e xānevādegi	نام خانوادگی

postage rate	ta'refe	تعرفه
standard (adj)	ādi	عادی
economical (adj)	ādi	عادی

weight	vazn	وزن
to weigh (~ letters)	vazn kardan	وزن کردن

envelope	pākat	پاکت
postage stamp	tambr	تمبر
to stamp an envelope	tamr zadan	تمبر زدن

43. Banking

bank	bānk	بانک
branch (of bank, etc.)	šo'be	شعبه
bank clerk, consultant	mošāver	مشاور
manager (director)	modir	مدیر
bank account	hesāb-e bānki	حساب بانکی
account number	šomāre-ye hesāb	شمارۀ حساب
checking account	hesāb-e jāri	حساب جاری
savings account	hesāb-e pasandāz	حساب پس انداز
to open an account	hesāb-e bāz kardan	حساب باز کردن
to close the account	hesāb rā bastan	حساب را بستن
to deposit into the account	be hesāb rixtan	به حساب ریختن
to withdraw (vt)	az hesāb bardāštan	از حساب برداشتن
deposit	seporde	سپرده
to make a deposit	seporde gozāštan	سپرده گذاشتن
wire transfer	enteqāl	انتقال
to wire, to transfer	enteqāl dādan	انتقال دادن
sum	jam'-e kol	جمع کل
How much?	čeqadr?	چقدر؟
signature	emzā'	امضاء
to sign (vt)	emzā kardan	امضا کردن
credit card	kārt-e e'tebāri	کارت اعتباری
code (PIN code)	kod	کد
credit card number	šomāre-ye kārt-e e'tebāri	شماره کارت اعتباری
ATM	xodpardāz	خودپرداز
check	ček	چک
to write a check	ček neveštan	چک نوشتن
checkbook	daste-ye ček	دسته چک
loan (bank ~)	e'tebār	اعتبار
to apply for a loan	darxāst-e vam kardan	درخواست وام کردن
to get a loan	vām gereftan	وام گرفتن
to give a loan	vām dādan	وام دادن
guarantee	zemānat	ضمانت

44. Telephone. Phone conversation

telephone	telefon	تلفن
cell phone	telefon-e hamrāh	تلفن همراه
answering machine	monši-ye telefoni	منشی تلفنی
to call (by phone)	telefon zadan	تلفن زدن
phone call	tamās-e telefoni	تماس تلفنی
to dial a number	šomāre gereftan	شماره گرفتن
Hello!	alo!	الو!
to ask (vt)	porsidan	پرسیدن
to answer (vi, vt)	javāb dādan	جواب دادن
to hear (vt)	šenidan	شنیدن
well (adv)	xub	خوب
not well (adv)	bad	بد
noises (interference)	sedā	صدا
receiver	guši	گوشی
to pick up (~ the phone)	guši rā bar dāštan	گوشی را برداشتن
to hang up (~ the phone)	guši rā gozāštan	گوشی را گذاشتن
busy (engaged)	mašqul	مشغول
to ring (ab. phone)	zang zadan	زنگ زدن
telephone book	daftar-e telefon	دفتر تلفن
local (adj)	mahalli	محلی
local call	telefon-e dāxeli	تلفن داخلی
long distance (~ call)	beyn-e šahri	بین شهری
long-distance call	telefon-e beyn-e šahri	تلفن بین شهری
international (adj)	beynolmelali	بین المللی
international call	telefon-e beynolmelali	تلفن بین المللی

45. Cell phone

cell phone	telefon-e hamrāh	تلفن همراه
display	namāyešgar	نمایشگر
button	dokme	دکمه
SIM card	sim-e kārt	سیم کارت
battery	bātri	باطری
to be dead (battery)	tamām šodan bātri	تمام شدن باتری
charger	šāržer	شارژ
menu	meno	منو
settings	tanzimāt	تنظیمات
tune (melody)	āhang	آهنگ
to select (vt)	entexāb kardan	انتخاب کردن

calculator	māšin-e hesāb	ماشین حساب
voice mail	monši-ye telefoni	منشی تلفنی
alarm clock	sā'at-e zang dār	ساعت زنگ دار
contacts	daftar-e telefon	دفتر تلفن

| SMS (text message) | payāmak | پیامک |
| subscriber | moštarek | مشترک |

46. Stationery

| ballpoint pen | xodkār | خودکار |
| fountain pen | xodnevis | خودنویس |

pencil	medād	مداد
highlighter	māžik	ماژیک
felt-tip pen	māžik	ماژیک

| notepad | daftar-e yāddāšt | دفتر یادداشت |
| agenda (diary) | daftar-e yāddāšt | دفتر یادداشت |

ruler	xat keš	خط کش
calculator	māšin-e hesāb	ماشین حساب
eraser	pāk kon	پاک کن
thumbtack	punez	پونز
paper clip	gire	گیره

glue	časb	چسب
stapler	mangane-ye zan	منگنه زن
hole punch	pānč	پانچ
pencil sharpener	madād-e tarāš	مداد تراش

47. Foreign languages

language	zabān	زبان
foreign (adj)	xāreji	خارجی
foreign language	zabān-e xāreji	زبان خارجی
to study (vt)	dars xāndan	درس خواندن
to learn (language, etc.)	yād gereftan	یاد گرفتن

to read (vi, vt)	xāndan	خواندن
to speak (vi, vt)	harf zadan	حرف زدن
to understand (vt)	fahmidan	فهمیدن
to write (vt)	neveštan	نوشتن

fast (adv)	sari'	سریع
slowly (adv)	āheste	آهسته
fluently (adv)	ravān	روان
rules	qavā'ed	قواعد

grammar	gerāmer	گرامر
vocabulary	vājegān	واژگان
phonetics	āvā-šenāsi	آواشناسی

textbook	ketāb-e darsi	کتاب درسی
dictionary	farhang-e loqat	فرهنگ لغت
teach-yourself book	xod-āmuz	خودآموز
phrasebook	ketāb-e mokāleme	کتاب مکالمه

cassette, tape	kāst	کاست
videotape	kāst-e video	کاست ویدئو
CD, compact disc	si-di	سیدی
DVD	dey vey dey	دی وی دی

alphabet	alefbā	الفبا
to spell (vt)	heji kardan	هجی کردن
pronunciation	talaffoz	تلفظ

accent	lahje	لهجه
with an accent	bā lahje	با لهجه
without an accent	bi lahje	بی لهجه

| word | kalame | کلمه |
| meaning | ma'ni | معنی |

course (e.g., a French ~)	dowre	دوره
to sign up	nām-nevisi kardan	نام نویسی کردن
teacher	ostād	استاد

translation (process)	tarjome	ترجمه
translation (text, etc.)	tarjome	ترجمه
translator	motarjem	مترجم
interpreter	motarjem-e šafāhi	مترجم شفاهی

| polyglot | čand zabāni | چند زبانی |
| memory | hāfeze | حافظه |

MEALS. RESTAURANT

48. Table setting

spoon	qāšoq	قاشق
knife	kārd	کارد
fork	čangāl	چنگال
cup (e.g., coffee ~)	fenjān	فنجان
plate (dinner ~)	bošqāb	بشقاب
saucer	na'lbeki	نعلبکی
napkin (on table)	dastmāl	دستمال
toothpick	xelāl-e dandān	خلال دندان

49. Restaurant

restaurant	resturān	رستوران
coffee house	kāfe	کافه
pub, bar	bār	بار
tearoom	qahve xāne	قهوه خانه
waiter	pišxedmat	پیشخدمت
waitress	pišxedmat	پیشخدمت
bartender	motesaddi-ye bār	متصدی بار
menu	meno	منو
wine list	kārt-e šarāb	کارت شراب
to book a table	miz rezerv kardan	میز رزرو کردن
course, dish	qazā	غذا
to order (meal)	sefāreš dādan	سفارش دادن
to make an order	sefāreš dādan	سفارش دادن
aperitif	mašrub-e piš qazā	مشروب پیش غذا
appetizer	piš qazā	پیش غذا
dessert	deser	دسر
check	surat hesāb	صورت حساب
to pay the check	surat-e hesāb rā pardāxtan	صورت حساب را پرداختن
to give change	baqiye rā dādan	بقیه را دادن
tip	an'ām	انعام

50. Meals

| food | qazā | غذا |
| to eat (vi, vt) | xordan | خوردن |

breakfast	sobhāne	صبحانه
to have breakfast	sobhāne xordan	صبحانه خوردن
lunch	nāhār	ناهار
to have lunch	nāhār xordan	ناهار خوردن
dinner	šām	شام
to have dinner	šām xordan	شام خوردن

| appetite | eštehā | اشتها |
| Enjoy your meal! | nuš-e jān | نوش جان |

to open (~ a bottle)	bāz kardan	باز کردن
to spill (liquid)	rixtan	ریختن
to spill out (vi)	rixtan	ریختن

to boil (vi)	jušidan	جوشیدن
to boil (vt)	jušāndan	جوشاندن
boiled (~ water)	jušide	جوشیده
to chill, cool down (vt)	sard kardan	سرد کردن
to chill (vi)	sard šodan	سرد شدن

| taste, flavor | maze | مزه |
| aftertaste | maze | مزه |

to slim down (lose weight)	lāqar kardan	لاغر کردن
diet	režim	رژیم
vitamin	vitāmin	ویتامین
calorie	kālori	کالری
vegetarian (n)	giyāh xār	گیاه خوار
vegetarian (adj)	giyāh xāri	گیاه خواری

fats (nutrient)	čarbi-hā	چربی ها
proteins	porotein	پروتئین
carbohydrates	karbohidrāt-hā	کربو هیدرات ها

slice (of lemon, ham)	qet'e	قطعه
piece (of cake, pie)	tekke	تکه
crumb (of bread, cake, etc.)	zarre	ذره

51. Cooked dishes

course, dish	qazā	غذا
cuisine	qazā	غذا
recipe	dastur-e poxt	دستور پخت

portion	pors	پرس
salad	sālād	سالاد
soup	sup	سوپ
clear soup (broth)	pāye-ye sup	پایه سوپ
sandwich (bread)	sāndevič	ساندویچ
fried eggs	nimru	نیمرو
hamburger (beefburger)	hamberger	همبرگر
beefsteak	esteyk	استیک
side dish	moxallafāt	مخلفات
spaghetti	espāgeti	اسپاگتی
mashed potatoes	pure-ye sibi zamini	پورهٔ سیب زمینی
pizza	pitzā	پیتزا
porridge (oatmeal, etc.)	šurbā	شوربا
omelet	ommol-at	املت
boiled (e.g., ~ beef)	āb paz	آب پز
smoked (adj)	dudi	دودی
fried (adj)	sorx šode	سرخ شده
dried (adj)	xošk	خشک
frozen (adj)	yax zade	یخ زده
pickled (adj)	torši	ترشی
sweet (sugary)	širin	شیرین
salty (adj)	šur	شور
cold (adj)	sard	سرد
hot (adj)	dāq	داغ
bitter (adj)	talx	تلخ
tasty (adj)	xoš mazze	خوش مزه
to cook in boiling water	poxtan	پختن
to cook (dinner)	poxtan	پختن
to fry (vt)	sorx kardan	سرخ کردن
to heat up (food)	garm kardan	گرم کردن
to salt (vt)	namak zadan	نمک زدن
to pepper (vt)	felfel pāšidan	فلفل پاشیدن
to grate (vt)	rande kardan	رنده کردن
peel (n)	pust	پوست
to peel (vt)	pust kandan	پوست کندن

52. Food

meat	gušt	گوشت
chicken	morq	مرغ
Rock Cornish hen (poussin)	juje	جوجه
duck	ordak	اردک

goose	qāz	غاز
game	gušt-e šekār	گوشت شکار
turkey	gušt-e buqalamun	گوشت بوقلمون
pork	gušt-e xuk	گوشت خوک
veal	gušt-e gusāle	گوشت گوساله
lamb	gušt-e gusfand	گوشت گوسفند
beef	gušt-e gāv	گوشت گاو
rabbit	xarguš	خرگوش
sausage (bologna, pepperoni, etc.)	kālbās	کالباس
vienna sausage (frankfurter)	sosis	سوسیس
bacon	beykon	بیکن
ham	žāmbon	ژامبون
gammon	rān xuk	ران خوک
pâté	pāte	پاته
liver	jegar	جگر
hamburger (ground beef)	hamberger	همبرگر
tongue	zabān	زبان
egg	toxm-e morq	تخم مرغ
eggs	toxm-e morq-ha	تخم مرغ ها
egg white	sefide-ye toxm-e morq	سفیده تخم مرغ
egg yolk	zarde-ye toxm-e morq	زرده تخم مرغ
fish	māhi	ماهی
seafood	qazā-ye daryāyi	غذای دریایی
crustaceans	saxtpustān	سختپوستان
caviar	xāviār	خاویار
crab	xarčang	خرچنگ
shrimp	meygu	میگو
oyster	sadaf-e xorāki	صدف خوراکی
spiny lobster	xarčang-e xārdār	خرچنگ خاردار
octopus	hašt pā	هشت پا
squid	māhi-ye morakkab	ماهی مرکب
sturgeon	māhi-ye xāviār	ماهی خاویار
salmon	māhi-ye salemon	ماهی سالمون
halibut	halibut	هالیبوت
cod	māhi-ye rowqan	ماهی روغن
mackerel	māhi-ye esqumeri	ماهی اسقومری
tuna	tan māhi	تن ماهی
eel	mārmāhi	مارماهی
trout	māhi-ye qezelālā	ماهی قزل آلا
sardine	sārdin	ساردین
pike	ordak māhi	اردک ماهی

herring	māhi-ye šur	ماهی شور
bread	nān	نان
cheese	panir	پنیر
sugar	qand	قند
salt	namak	نمک

rice	berenj	برنج
pasta (macaroni)	mākāroni	ماکارونی
noodles	rešte-ye farangi	رشته فرنگی

butter	kare	کره
vegetable oil	rowqan-e nabāti	روغن نباتی
sunflower oil	rowqan āftābgardān	روغن آفتاب گردان
margarine	mārgārin	مارگارین

| olives | zeytun | زیتون |
| olive oil | rowqan-e zeytun | روغن زیتون |

milk	šir	شیر
condensed milk	šir-e čegāl	شیر چگال
yogurt	mās-at	ماست
sour cream	xāme-ye torš	خامة ترش
cream (of milk)	saršir	سرشیر

| mayonnaise | māyonez | مایونز |
| buttercream | xāme | خامه |

cereal grains (wheat, etc.)	hobubāt	حبوبات
flour	ārd	آرد
canned food	konserv-hā	کنسرو ها

cornflakes	bereštuk	برشتوک
honey	asal	عسل
jam	morabbā	مربا
chewing gum	ādāms	آدامس

53. Drinks

water	āb	آب
drinking water	āb-e āšāmidani	آب آشامیدنی
mineral water	āb-e ma'dani	آب معدنی

still (adj)	bedun-e gāz	بدون گاز
carbonated (adj)	gāzdār	گازدار
sparkling (adj)	gāzdār	گازدار
ice	yax	یخ
with ice	yax dār	یخ دار

| non-alcoholic (adj) | bi alkol | بی الکل |
| soft drink | nušābe-ye bi alkol | نوشابهٔ بی الکل |

| refreshing drink | nušābe-ye xonak | نوشابهٔ خنک |
| lemonade | limunād | لیموناد |

liquors	mašrubāt-e alkoli	مشروبات الکلی
wine	šarāb	شراب
white wine	šarāb-e sefid	شراب سفید
red wine	šarāb-e sorx	شراب سرخ

liqueur	likor	لیکور
champagne	šāmpāyn	شامپاین
vermouth	vermut	ورموت

whiskey	viski	ویسکی
vodka	vodkā	ودکا
gin	jin	جین
cognac	konyāk	کنیاک
rum	araq-e neyšekar	عرق نیشکر

coffee	qahve	قهوه
black coffee	qahve-ye talx	قهوهٔ تلخ
coffee with milk	šir-qahve	شیرقهوه
cappuccino	kāpočino	کاپوچینو
instant coffee	qahve-ye fowri	قهوه فوری

milk	šir	شیر
cocktail	kuktel	کوکتل
milkshake	kuktele šir	کوکتل شیر

juice	āb-e mive	آب میوه
tomato juice	āb-e gowjefarangi	آب گوجه فرنگی
orange juice	āb-e porteqāl	آب پرتقال
freshly squeezed juice	āb-e mive-ye taze	آب میوهٔ تازه

beer	ābejow	آبجو
light beer	ābejow-ye sabok	آبجوی سبک
dark beer	ābejow-ye tire	آبجوی تیره

tea	čāy	چای
black tea	čāy-e siyāh	چای سیاه
green tea	čāy-e sabz	چای سبز

54. Vegetables

| vegetables | sabzijāt | سبزیجات |
| greens | sabzi | سبزی |

tomato	gowje farangi	گوجه فرنگی
cucumber	xiyār	خیار
carrot	havij	هویج
potato	sib zamini	سیب زمینی

| onion | piyāz | پیاز |
| garlic | sir | سیر |

cabbage	kalam	کلم
cauliflower	gol kalam	گل کلم
Brussels sprouts	koll-am boruksel	کلم بروکسل
broccoli	kalam borokli	کلم بروکلی

beetroot	čoqondar	چغندر
eggplant	bādenjān	بادنجان
zucchini	kadu sabz	کدو سبز
pumpkin	kadu tanbal	کدو تنبل
turnip	šalqam	شلغم

parsley	ja'fari	جعفری
dill	šavid	شوید
lettuce	kāhu	کاهو
celery	karafs	کرفس
asparagus	mārčube	مارچوبه
spinach	esfenāj	اسفناج

pea	noxod	نخود
beans	lubiyā	لوبیا
corn (maize)	zorrat	ذرت
kidney bean	lubiyā qermez	لوبیا قرمز

bell pepper	felfel	فلفل
radish	torobče	تربچه
artichoke	kangar farangi	کنگرفرنگی

55. Fruits. Nuts

fruit	mive	میوه
apple	sib	سیب
pear	golābi	گلابی
lemon	limu	لیمو
orange	porteqāl	پرتقال
strawberry (garden ~)	tut-e farangi	توت فرنگی

mandarin	nārengi	نارنگی
plum	ālu	آلو
peach	holu	هلو
apricot	zardālu	زردآلو
raspberry	tamešk	تمشک
pineapple	ānānās	آناناس

banana	mowz	موز
watermelon	hendevāne	هندوانه
grape	angur	انگور
sour cherry	ālbālu	آلبالو

sweet cherry	gilās	گیلاس
melon	xarboze	خربزه
grapefruit	gerip forut	گریپ فوروت
avocado	āvokādo	اووکادو
papaya	pāpāyā	پاپایا
mango	anbe	انبه
pomegranate	anār	انار
redcurrant	angur-e farangi-ye sorx	انگور فرنگی سرخ
blackcurrant	angur-e farangi-ye siyāh	انگور فرنگی سیاه
gooseberry	angur-e farangi	انگور فرنگی
bilberry	zoqāl axte	زغال اخته
blackberry	šāh tut	شاه توت
raisin	kešmeš	کشمش
fig	anjir	انجیر
date	xormā	خرما
peanut	bādām zamin-i	بادام زمینی
almond	bādām	بادام
walnut	gerdu	گردو
hazelnut	fandoq	فندق
coconut	nārgil	نارگیل
pistachios	peste	پسته

56. Bread. Candy

bakers' confectionery (pastry)	širini jāt	شیرینی جات
bread	nān	نان
cookies	biskuit	بیسکوییت
chocolate (n)	šokolāt	شکلات
chocolate (as adj)	šokolāti	شکلاتی
candy (wrapped)	āb nabāt	آب نبات
cake (e.g., cupcake)	nān-e širini	نان شیرینی
cake (e.g., birthday ~)	širini	شیرینی
pie (e.g., apple ~)	keyk	کیک
filling (for cake, pie)	čāšni	چاشنی
jam (whole fruit jam)	morabbā	مربا
marmalade	mārmālād	مارمالاد
waffles	vāfel	وافل
ice-cream	bastani	بستنی
pudding	puding	پودینگ

57. Spices

salt	namak	نمک
salty (adj)	šur	شور
to salt (vt)	namak zadan	نمک زدن
black pepper	felfel-e siyāh	فلفل سیاه
red pepper (milled ~)	felfel-e sorx	فلفل سرخ
mustard	xardal	خردل
horseradish	torob-e kuhi	ترب کوهی
condiment	adviye	ادویه
spice	adviye	ادویه
sauce	ses	سس
vinegar	serke	سرکه
anise	rāziyāne	رازیانه
basil	reyhān	ریحان
cloves	mixak	میخک
ginger	zanjefil	زنجفیل
coriander	gešniz	گشنیز
cinnamon	dārčin	دارچین
sesame	konjed	کنجد
bay leaf	barg-e bu	برگ بو
paprika	paprika	پاپریکا
caraway	zire	زیره
saffron	za'ferān	زعفران

PERSONAL INFORMATION. FAMILY

58. Personal information. Forms

name (first name)	esm	اسم
surname (last name)	nām-e xānevādegi	نام خانوادگی
date of birth	tārix-e tavallod	تاریخ تولد
place of birth	mahall-e tavallod	محل تولد
nationality	melliyat	ملیت
place of residence	mahall-e sokunat	محل سکونت
country	kešvar	کشور
profession (occupation)	šoql	شغل
gender, sex	jens	جنس
height	qad	قد
weight	vazn	وزن

59. Family members. Relatives

mother	mādar	مادر
father	pedar	پدر
son	pesar	پسر
daughter	doxtar	دختر
younger daughter	doxtar-e kučak	دختر کوچک
younger son	pesar-e kučak	پسر کوچک
eldest daughter	doxtar-e bozorg	دختر بزرگ
eldest son	pesar-e bozorg	پسر بزرگ
brother	barādar	برادر
elder brother	barādar-e bozorg	برادر بزرگ
younger brother	barādar-e kučak	برادر کوچک
sister	xāhar	خواهر
elder sister	xāhar-e bozorg	خواهر بزرگ
younger sister	xāhar-e kučak	خواهر کوچک
cousin (masc.)	pesar 'amu	پسر عمو
cousin (fem.)	doxtar amu	دختر عمو
mom, mommy	māmān	مامان
dad, daddy	bābā	بابا
parents	vāledeyn	والدین
child	kudak	کودک
children	bače-hā	بچه ها

grandmother	mādarbozorg	مادربزرگ
grandfather	pedar-bozorg	پدربزرگ
grandson	nave	نوه
granddaughter	nave	نوه
grandchildren	nave-hā	نوه ها
uncle	amu	عمو
aunt	xāle yā amme	خاله یا عمه
nephew	barādar-zāde	برادرزاده
niece	xāhar-zāde	خواهرزاده
mother-in-law (wife's mother)	mādarzan	مادرزن
father-in-law (husband's father)	pedar-šowhar	پدرشوهر
son-in-law (daughter's husband)	dāmād	داماد
stepmother	nāmādari	نامادری
stepfather	nāpedari	ناپدری
infant	nowzād	نوزاد
baby (infant)	širxār	شیرخوار
little boy, kid	pesar-e kučulu	پسر کوچولو
wife	zan	زن
husband	šowhar	شوهر
spouse (husband)	hamsar	همسر
spouse (wife)	hamsar	همسر
married (masc.)	mote'ahhel	متأهل
married (fem.)	mote'ahhel	متأهل
single (unmarried)	mojarrad	مجرد
bachelor	mojarrad	مجرد
divorced (masc.)	talāq gerefte	طلاق گرفته
widow	bive zan	بیوه زن
widower	bive	بیوه
relative	xišāvand	خویشاوند
close relative	aqvām-e nazdik	اقوام نزدیک
distant relative	aqvām-e dur	اقوام دور
relatives	aqvām	اقوام
orphan (boy or girl)	yatim	یتیم
guardian (of a minor)	qayyem	قیم
to adopt (a boy)	be pesari gereftan	به پسری گرفتن
to adopt (a girl)	be doxtari gereftan	به دختری گرفتن

60. Friends. Coworkers

friend (masc.)	dust	دوست
friend (fem.)	dust	دوست

friendship	dusti	دوستی
to be friends	dust budan	دوست بودن
buddy (masc.)	rafiq	رفیق
buddy (fem.)	rafiq	رفیق
partner	šarik	شریک
chief (boss)	ra'is	رئیس
superior (n)	ra'is	رئیس
owner, proprietor	sāheb	صاحب
subordinate (n)	zirdast	زیردست
colleague	hamkār	همکار
acquaintance (person)	āšnā	آشنا
fellow traveler	hamsafar	همسفر
classmate	ham kelās	هم کلاس
neighbor (masc.)	hamsāye	همسایه
neighbor (fem.)	hamsāye	همسایه
neighbors	hamsāye-hā	همسایه ها

HUMAN BODY. MEDICINE

61. Head

head	sar	سر
face	surat	صورت
nose	bini	بینی
mouth	dahān	دهان
eye	češm	چشم
eyes	češm-hā	چشم ها
pupil	mardomak	مردمک
eyebrow	abru	ابرو
eyelash	može	مژه
eyelid	pelek	پلک
tongue	zabān	زبان
tooth	dandān	دندان
lips	lab-hā	لب ها
cheekbones	ostexānhā-ye gune	استخوان های گونه
gum	lase	لثه
palate	saqf-e dahān	سقف دهان
nostrils	surāxhā-ye bini	سوراخ های بینی
chin	čāne	چانه
jaw	fak	فک
cheek	gune	گونه
forehead	pišāni	پیشانی
temple	gijgāh	گیجگاه
ear	guš	گوش
back of the head	pas gardan	پس گردن
neck	gardan	گردن
throat	galu	گلو
hair	mu-hā	مو ها
hairstyle	model-e mu	مدل مو
haircut	model-e mu	مدل مو
wig	kolāh-e gis	کلاه گیس
mustache	sebil	سبیل
beard	riš	ریش
to have (a beard, etc.)	gozāštan	گذاشتن
braid	muy-ye bāfte	موی بافته
sideburns	xatt-e riš	خط ریش
red-haired (adj)	muqermez	موقرمز

gray (hair)	sefid-e mu	سفید مو
bald (adj)	tās	طاس
bald patch	tāsi	طاسی

| ponytail | dom-e asbi | دم اسبی |
| bangs | čatri | چتری |

62. Human body

| hand | dast | دست |
| arm | bāzu | بازو |

finger	angošt	انگشت
toe	šast-e pā	شصت پا
thumb	šost	شست
little finger	angošt-e kučak	انگشت کرچک
nail	nāxon	ناخن

fist	mošt	مشت
palm	kaf-e dast	کف دست
wrist	moč-e dast	مچ دست
forearm	sā'ed	ساعد
elbow	āranj	آرنج
shoulder	ketf	کتف

leg	pā	پا
foot	pā	پا
knee	zānu	زانو
calf (part of leg)	sāq	ساق
hip	rān	ران
heel	pāšne-ye pā	پاشنهٔ پا

body	badan	بدن
stomach	šekam	شکم
chest	sine	سینه
breast	sine	سینه
flank	pahlu	پهلو
back	pošt	پشت
lower back	kamar	کمر
waist	dur-e kamar	دور کمر

navel (belly button)	nāf	ناف
buttocks	nešiman-e gāh	نشیمن گاه
bottom	bāsan	باسن

beauty mark	xāl	خال
birthmark (café au lait spot)	xāl-e mādarzād	خال مادرزاد
tattoo	xāl kubi	خال کوبی
scar	jā-ye zaxm	جای زخم

63. Diseases

sickness	bimāri	بیماری
to be sick	bimār budan	بیمار بودن
health	salāmati	سلامتی

runny nose (coryza)	āb-e rizeš-e bini	آب ریزش بینی
tonsillitis	varam-e lowze	ورم لوزه
cold (illness)	sarmā xordegi	سرما خوردگی
to catch a cold	sarmā xordan	سرما خوردن

bronchitis	boronšit	برنشیت
pneumonia	zātorrie	ذات الریه
flu, influenza	ānfolānzā	آنفولانزا

nearsighted (adj)	nazdik bin	نزدیک بین
farsighted (adj)	durbin	دوربین
strabismus (crossed eyes)	enherāf-e čašm	انحراف چشم
cross-eyed (adj)	luč	لوچ
cataract	āb morvārid	آب مروارید
glaucoma	ab-e siyāh	آب سیاه

stroke	sekte-ye maqzi	سکته مغزی
heart attack	sekte-ye qalbi	سکته قلبی
myocardial infarction	ānfārktus	آنفارکتوس
paralysis	falaji	فلجی
to paralyze (vt)	falj kardan	فلج کردن

allergy	ālerži	آلرژی
asthma	āsm	آسم
diabetes	diyābet	دیابت

| toothache | dandān-e dard | دندان درد |
| caries | pusidegi | پوسیدگی |

diarrhea	eshāl	اسهال
constipation	yobusat	یبوست
stomach upset	nārāhati-ye me'de	ناراحتی معده
food poisoning	masmumiyat	مسمومیت
to get food poisoning	masmum šodan	مسموم شدن

arthritis	varam-e mafāsel	ورم مفاصل
rickets	rāšitism	راشیتیسم
rheumatism	romātism	روماتیسم
atherosclerosis	tasallob-e šarāin	تصلب شرائین

gastritis	varam-e me'de	ورم معده
appendicitis	āpāndisit	آپاندیسیت
cholecystitis	eltehāb-e kise-ye safrā	التهاب کیسه صفرا
ulcer	zaxm	زخم
measles	sorxak	سرخک

rubella (German measles)	sorxje	سرخجه
jaundice	yaraqān	یرقان
hepatitis	hepātit	هپاتیت
schizophrenia	šizoferni	شیزوفرنی
rabies (hydrophobia)	hāri	هاری
neurosis	extelāl-e aʻsāb	اختلال اعصاب
concussion	zarbe-ye maqzi	ضربه مغزی
cancer	saratān	سرطان
sclerosis	eskeleroz	اسکلروز
multiple sclerosis	eskeleroz čandgāne	اسکلروز چندگانه
alcoholism	alkolism	الکلیسم
alcoholic (n)	alkoli	الکلی
syphilis	siflis	سیفلیس
AIDS	eydz	ایدز
tumor	tumor	تومور
malignant (adj)	bad xim	بد خیم
benign (adj)	xoš xim	خوش خیم
fever	tab	تب
malaria	mālāriyā	مالاریا
gangrene	qānqāriyā	قانقاریا
seasickness	daryā-zadegi	دریازدگی
epilepsy	sarʻ	صرع
epidemic	epidemi	اپیدمی
typhus	hasbe	حصبه
tuberculosis	sel	سل
cholera	vabā	وبا
plague (bubonic ~)	tāʻun	طاعون

64. Symptoms. Treatments. Part 1

symptom	alāem-e bimāri	علائم بیماری
temperature	damā	دما
high temperature (fever)	tab	تب
pulse	nabz	نبض
dizziness (vertigo)	sargije	سرگیجه
hot (adj)	dāq	داغ
shivering	raʻše	رعشه
pale (e.g., ~ face)	rang paride	رنگ پریده
cough	sorfe	سرفه
to cough (vi)	sorfe kardan	سرفه کردن
to sneeze (vi)	atse kardan	عطسه کردن
faint	qaš	غش

to faint (vi)	qaš kardan	غش کردن
bruise (hématome)	kabudi	کبودی
bump (lump)	barāmadegi	برآمدگی
to bang (bump)	barxord kardan	برخورد کردن
contusion (bruise)	kuftegi	کوفتگی
to get a bruise	zarb didan	ضرب دیدن
to limp (vi)	langidan	لنگیدن
dislocation	dar raftegi	دررفتگی
to dislocate (vt)	dar raftan	دررفتن
fracture	šekastegi	شکستگی
to have a fracture	dočār-e šekastegi šodan	دچار شکستگی شدن
cut (e.g., paper ~)	boridegi	بریدگی
to cut oneself	boridan	بریدن
bleeding	xunrizi	خونریزی
burn (injury)	suxtegi	سوختگی
to get burned	dočār-e suxtegi šodan	دچار سوختگی شدن
to prick (vt)	surāx kardan	سوراخ کردن
to prick oneself	surāx kardan	سوراخ کردن
to injure (vt)	āsib resāndan	آسیب رساندن
injury	zaxm	زخم
wound	zaxm	زخم
trauma	zarbe	ضربه
to be delirious	hazyān goftan	هذیان گفتن
to stutter (vi)	loknat dāštan	لکنت داشتن
sunstroke	āftāb-zadegi	آفتاب‌زدگی

65. Symptoms. Treatments. Part 2

pain, ache	dard	درد
splinter (in foot, etc.)	xār	خار
sweat (perspiration)	araq	عرق
to sweat (perspire)	araq kardan	عرق کردن
vomiting	estefrāq	استفراغ
convulsions	tašannoj	تشنج
pregnant (adj)	bārdār	باردار
to be born	motevalled šodan	متولد شدن
delivery, labor	vaz'-e haml	وضع حمل
to deliver (~ a baby)	be donyā āvardan	به دنیا آوردن
abortion	seqt-e janin	سقط جنین
breathing, respiration	tanaffos	تنفس
in-breath (inhalation)	estenšāq	استنشاق
out-breath (exhalation)	bāzdam	بازدم

to exhale (breathe out)	bāzdamidan	بازدمیدن
to inhale (vi)	nafas kešidan	نفس کشیدن
disabled person	ma'lul	معلول
cripple	falaj	فلج
drug addict	mo'tād	معتاد
deaf (adj)	kar	کر
mute (adj)	lāl	لال
deaf mute (adj)	kar-o lāl	کر و لال
mad, insane (adj)	divāne	دیوانه
madman (demented person)	divāne	دیوانه
madwoman	divāne	دیوانه
to go insane	divāne šodan	دیوانه شدن
gene	žen	ژن
immunity	masuniyat	مصونیت
hereditary (adj)	mowrusi	موروثی
congenital (adj)	mādarzād	مادرزاد
virus	virus	ویروس
microbe	mikrob	میکروب
bacterium	bākteri	باکتری
infection	ofunat	عفونت

66. Symptoms. Treatments. Part 3

hospital	bimārestān	بیمارستان
patient	bimār	بیمار
diagnosis	tašxis	تشخیص
cure	mo'āleje	معالجه
medical treatment	darmān	درمان
to get treatment	darmān šodan	درمان شدن
to treat (~ a patient)	mo'āleje kardan	معالجه کردن
to nurse (look after)	parastāri kardan	پرستاری کردن
care (nursing ~)	parastāri	پرستاری
operation, surgery	amal-e jarrāhi	عمل جراحی
to bandage (head, limb)	pānsemān kardan	پانسمان کردن
bandaging	pānsemān	پانسمان
vaccination	vāksināsyon	واکسیناسیون
to vaccinate (vt)	vāksine kardan	واکسینه کردن
injection, shot	tazriq	تزریق
to give an injection	tazriq kardan	تزریق کردن
attack	hamle	حمله
amputation	qat'-e ozv	قطع عضو

to amputate (vt)	qat' kardan	قطع کردن
coma	komā	کما
to be in a coma	dar komā budan	در کما بودن
intensive care	morāqebat-e viže	مراقبت ویژه
to recover (~ from flu)	behbud yāftan	بهبود یافتن
condition (patient's ~)	hālat	حالت
consciousness	huš	هوش
memory (faculty)	hāfeze	حافظه
to pull out (tooth)	dandān kešidan	دندان کشیدن
filling	por kardan	پر کردن
to fill (a tooth)	por kardan	پر کردن
hypnosis	hipnotizm	هیپنوتیزم
to hypnotize (vt)	hipnotizm kardan	هیپنوتیزم کردن

67. Medicine. Drugs. Accessories

medicine, drug	dāru	دارو
remedy	darmān	درمان
to prescribe (vt)	tajviz kardan	تجویز کردن
prescription	nosxe	نسخه
tablet, pill	qors	قرص
ointment	pomād	پماد
ampule	āmpul	آمپول
mixture	šarbat	شربت
syrup	šarbat	شربت
pill	kapsul	کپسول
powder	pudr	پودر
gauze bandage	bānd	باند
cotton wool	panbe	پنبه
iodine	yod	ید
Band-Aid	časb-e zaxm	چسب زخم
eyedropper	qatre čekān	قطره چکان
thermometer	damāsanj	دماسنج
syringe	sorang	سرنگ
wheelchair	vilčer	ویلچر
crutches	čub zir baqal	چوب زیر بغل
painkiller	mosaken	مسکن
laxative	moshel	مسهل
spirits (ethanol)	alkol	الکل
medicinal herbs	giyāhān-e dāruyi	گیاهان دارویی
herbal (~ tea)	giyāhi	گیاهی

APARTMENT

68. Apartment

apartment	āpārtemān	آپارتمان
room	otāq	اتاق
bedroom	otāq-e xāb	اتاق خواب
dining room	otāq-e qazāxori	اتاق غذاخوری
living room	mehmānxāne	مهمانخانه
study (home office)	daftar	دفتر
entry room	tālār-e vorudi	تالار ورودی
bathroom (room with a bath or shower)	hammām	حمام
half bath	tuālet	توالت
ceiling	saqf	سقف
floor	kaf	کف
corner	guše	گوشه

69. Furniture. Interior

furniture	mobl	مبل
table	miz	میز
chair	sandali	صندلی
bed	taxt-e xāb	تخت خواب
couch, sofa	kānāpe	کاناپه
armchair	mobl-e rāhati	مبل راحتی
bookcase	qafase-ye ketāb	قفسه کتاب
shelf	qafase	قفسه
wardrobe	komod	کمد
coat rack (wall-mounted ~)	raxt āviz	رخت آویز
coat stand	čub lebāsi	چوب لباسی
bureau, dresser	komod	کمد
coffee table	miz-e pišdasti	میز پیشدستی
mirror	āyene	آینه
carpet	farš	فرش
rug, small carpet	qāliče	قالیچه
fireplace	šumine	شومینه
candle	šam'	شمع

candlestick	šam'dān	شمعدان
drapes	parde	پرده
wallpaper	kāqaz-e divāri	کاغذ دیواری
blinds (jalousie)	kerkere	کرکره
table lamp	čerāq-e rumizi	چراغ رومیزی
wall lamp (sconce)	čerāq-e divāri	چراغ دیواری
floor lamp	ābāžur	آباژور
chandelier	luster	لوستر
leg (of chair, table)	pāye	پایه
armrest	daste-ye sandali	دستهٔ صندلی
back (backrest)	pošti	پشتی
drawer	kešow	کشو

70. Bedding

bedclothes	raxt-e xāb	رخت خواب
pillow	bālešt	بالشت
pillowcase	rubalešt	روبالشت
duvet, comforter	patu	پتو
sheet	malāfe	ملافه
bedspread	rutaxti	روتختی

71. Kitchen

kitchen	āšpazxāne	آشپزخانه
gas	gāz	گاز
gas stove (range)	ojāgh-e gāz	اجاق گاز
electric stove	ojāgh-e barghi	اجاق برقی
oven	fer	فر
microwave oven	māykrofer	مایکروفر
refrigerator	yaxčāl	یخچال
freezer	fereyzer	فریزر
dishwasher	māšin-e zarfšuyi	ماشین ظرفشویی
meat grinder	čarx-e gušt	چرخ گوشت
juicer	ābmive giri	آبمیوه گیری
toaster	towster	توستر
mixer	maxlut kon	مخلوط کن
coffee machine	qahve sāz	قهوه ساز
coffee pot	qahve juš	قهوه جوش
coffee grinder	āsiyāb-e qahve	آسیاب قهوه
kettle	ketri	کتری
teapot	quri	قوری

| lid | sarpuš | سرپوش |
| tea strainer | čāy sāf kon | چای صاف کن |

spoon	qāšoq	قاشق
teaspoon	qāšoq čāy xori	قاشق چای خوری
soup spoon	qāšoq sup xori	قاشق سوپ خوری
fork	čangāl	چنگال
knife	kārd	کارد

tableware (dishes)	zoruf	ظروف
plate (dinner ~)	bošqāb	بشقاب
saucer	na'lbeki	نعلبکی

shot glass	gilās-e vodkā	گیلاس ودکا
glass (tumbler)	estekān	استکان
cup	fenjān	فنجان

sugar bowl	qandān	قندان
salt shaker	namakdān	نمکدان
pepper shaker	felfeldān	فلفلدان
butter dish	zarf-e kare	ظرف کره

stock pot (soup pot)	qāblame	قابلمه
frying pan (skillet)	tābe	تابه
ladle	malāqe	ملاقه
colander	ābkeš	آبکش
tray (serving ~)	sini	سینی

bottle	botri	بطری
jar (glass)	šiše	شیشه
can	quti	قوطی

bottle opener	dar bāz kon	در بازکن
can opener	dar bāz kon	در بازکن
corkscrew	dar bāz kon	در بازکن
filter	filter	فیلتر
to filter (vt)	filter kardan	فیلتر کردن

| trash, garbage (food waste, etc.) | āšqāl | آشغال |
| trash can (kitchen ~) | satl-e zobāle | سطل زباله |

72. Bathroom

bathroom	hammām	حمام
water	āb	آب
faucet	šir	شیر
hot water	āb-e dāq	آب داغ
cold water	āb-e sard	آب سرد
toothpaste	xamir-e dandān	خمیر دندان

| to brush one's teeth | mesvāk zadan | مسواک زدن |
| toothbrush | mesvāk | مسواک |

to shave (vi)	riš tarāšidan	ریش تراشیدن
shaving foam	xamir-e eslāh	خمیر اصلاح
razor	tiq	تیغ

to wash (one's hands, etc.)	šostan	شستن
to take a bath	hamām kardan	حمام کردن
shower	duš	دوش
to take a shower	duš gereftan	دوش گرفتن

bathtub	vān hammām	وان حمام
toilet (toilet bowl)	tuālet-e farangi	توالت فرنگی
sink (washbasin)	sink	سینک

| soap | sābun | صابون |
| soap dish | jā sābun | جا صابون |

sponge	abr	ابر
shampoo	šāmpu	شامپو
towel	howle	حوله
bathrobe	howle-ye hamām	حوله حمام

laundry (process)	raxčuyi	لباسشویی
washing machine	māšin-e lebas-šui	ماشین لباسشویی
to do the laundry	šostan-e lebās	شستن لباس
laundry detergent	pudr-e lebas-šui	پودر لباسشویی

73. Household appliances

TV set	televiziyon	تلویزیون
tape recorder	zabt-e sowt	ضبط صوت
VCR (video recorder)	video	ویدئو
radio	rādiyo	رادیو
player (CD, MP3, etc.)	paxš konande	پخش کننده

video projector	video porožektor	ویدئو پروژکتور
home movie theater	sinamā-ye xānegi	سینمای خانگی
DVD player	paxš konande-ye di vi di	پخش کننده دی وی دی
amplifier	āmpli-fāyer	آمپلی فایر
video game console	konsul-e bāzi	کنسول بازی

video camera	durbin-e filmbardāri	دوربین فیلمبرداری
camera (photo)	durbin-e akkāsi	دوربین عکاسی
digital camera	durbin-e dijitāl	دوربین دیجیتال

vacuum cleaner	jāru barqi	جارو برقی
iron (e.g., steam ~)	oto	اتو
ironing board	miz-e oto	میز اتو

telephone	telefon	تلفن
cell phone	telefon-e hamrāh	تلفن همراه
typewriter	māšin-e tahrir	ماشین تحریر
sewing machine	čarx-e xayyāti	چرخ خیاطی

microphone	mikrofon	میکروفون
headphones	guši	گوشی
remote control (TV)	kontorol az rāh-e dur	کنترل از راه دور

CD, compact disc	si-di	سیدی
cassette, tape	kāst	کاست
vinyl record	safhe-ye gerāmāfon	صفحه گرامافون

THE EARTH. WEATHER

74. Outer space

space	fazā	فضا
space (as adj)	fazāyi	فضایی
outer space	fazā-ye keyhān	فضای کیهان
world	jahān	جهان
universe	giti	گیتی
galaxy	kahkešān	کهکشان
star	setāre	ستاره
constellation	surat-e falaki	صورت فلکی
planet	sayyāre	سیاره
satellite	māhvāre	ماهواره
meteorite	sang-e āsmāni	سنگ آسمانی
comet	setāre-ye donbāle dār	ستارهٔ دنباله دار
asteroid	šahāb	شهاب
orbit	madār	مدار
to revolve (~ around the Earth)	gardidan	گردیدن
atmosphere	jav	جو
the Sun	āftāb	آفتاب
solar system	manzume-ye šamsi	منظومه شمسی
solar eclipse	kosuf	کسوف
the Earth	zamin	زمین
the Moon	māh	ماه
Mars	merrix	مریخ
Venus	zahre	زهره
Jupiter	moštari	مشتری
Saturn	zohal	زحل
Mercury	atārod	عطارد
Uranus	orānus	اورانوس
Neptune	nepton	نپتون
Pluto	poloton	پلوتون
Milky Way	kahkešān rāh-e širi	کهکشان راه شیری
Great Bear (Ursa Major)	dobb-e akbar	دب اکبر
North Star	setāre-ye qotbi	ستاره قطبی

Martian	merrixi	مریخی
extraterrestrial (n)	farā zamini	فرا زمینی
alien	mowjud fazāyi	موجود فضایی
flying saucer	bošqāb-e parande	بشقاب پرنده

spaceship	fazā peymā	فضا پیما
space station	istgāh-e fazāyi	ایستگاه فضایی
blast-off	rāh andāzi	راه اندازی

engine	motor	موتور
nozzle	nāzel	نازل
fuel	suxt	سوخت

cockpit, flight deck	kābin	کابین
antenna	ānten	آنتن
porthole	panjere	پنجره
solar panel	bātri-ye xoršidi	باطری خورشیدی
spacesuit	lebās-e fazānavardi	لباس فضانوردی

| weightlessness | bi vazni | بی وزنی |
| oxygen | oksižen | اکسیژن |

| docking (in space) | vasl | وصل |
| to dock (vi, vt) | vasl kardan | وصل کردن |

observatory	rasadxāne	رصدخانه
telescope	teleskop	تلسکوپ
to observe (vt)	mošāhede kardan	مشاهده کردن
to explore (vt)	kašf kardan	کشف کردن

75. The Earth

the Earth	zamin	زمین
the globe (the Earth)	kare-ye zamin	کرۀ زمین
planet	sayyāre	سیاره

atmosphere	jav	جو
geography	joqrāfiyā	جغرافیا
nature	tabi'at	طبیعت

globe (table ~)	kare-ye joqrāfiyāyi	کرۀ جغرافیایی
map	naqše	نقشه
atlas	atlas	اطلس

Europe	orupā	اروپا
Asia	āsiyā	آسیا
Africa	āfriqā	آفریقا
Australia	ostorāliyā	استرالیا
America	emrikā	امریکا
North America	emrikā-ye šomāli	امریکای شمالی

South America	emrikā-ye jonubi	امریکای جنوبی
Antarctica	qotb-e jonub	قطب جنوب
the Arctic	qotb-e šomāl	قطب شمال

76. Cardinal directions

north	šomāl	شمال
to the north	be šomāl	به شمال
in the north	dar šomāl	در شمال
northern (adj)	šomāli	شمالی

south	jonub	جنوب
to the south	be jonub	به جنوب
in the south	dar jonub	در جنوب
southern (adj)	jonubi	جنوبی

west	qarb	غرب
to the west	be qarb	به غرب
in the west	dar qarb	در غرب
western (adj)	qarbi	غربی

east	šarq	شرق
to the east	be šarq	به شرق
in the east	dar šarq	در شرق
eastern (adj)	šarqi	شرقی

77. Sea. Ocean

sea	daryā	دریا
ocean	oqyānus	اقیانوس
gulf (bay)	xalij	خلیج
straits	tange	تنگه

| land (solid ground) | zamin | زمین |
| continent (mainland) | qāre | قاره |

island	jazire	جزیره
peninsula	šeb-e jazire	شبه جزیره
archipelago	majma'-ol-jazāyer	مجمع‌الجزایر

bay, cove	xalij-e kučak	خلیج کوچک
harbor	langargāh	لنگرگاه
lagoon	mordāb	مرداب
cape	damāqe	دماغه

atoll	jazire-ye marjāni	جزیره مرجانی
reef	tappe-ye daryāyi	تپه دریایی
coral	marjān	مرجان

coral reef	tappe-ye marjāni	تپه مرجانی
deep (adj)	amiq	عمیق
depth (deep water)	omq	عمق
abyss	partgāh	پرتگاه
trench (e.g., Mariana ~)	derāz godāl	درازگودال
current (Ocean ~)	jaryān	جریان
to surround (bathe)	ehāte kardan	احاطه کردن
shore	sāhel	ساحل
coast	sāhel	ساحل
flow (flood tide)	mod	مد
ebb (ebb tide)	jazr	جزر
shoal	sāhel-e šeni	ساحل شنی
bottom (~ of the sea)	qa'r	قعر
wave	mowj	موج
crest (~ of a wave)	nok	نوک
spume (sea foam)	kaf	کف
storm (sea storm)	tufān-e daryāyi	طوفان دریایی
hurricane	tufān	طوفان
tsunami	sonāmi	سونامی
calm (dead ~)	sokun-e daryā	سکون دریا
quiet, calm (adj)	ārām	آرام
pole	qotb	قطب
polar (adj)	qotbi	قطبی
latitude	arz-e joqrāfiyāyi	عرض جغرافیایی
longitude	tul-e joqrāfiyāyi	طول جغرافیایی
parallel	movāzi	موازی
equator	xatt-e ostavā	خط استوا
sky	āsemān	آسمان
horizon	ofoq	افق
air	havā	هوا
lighthouse	fānus-e daryāyi	فانوس دریایی
to dive (vi)	širje raftan	شیرجه رفتن
to sink (ab. boat)	qarq šodan	غرق شدن
treasures	ganj	گنج

78. Seas' and Oceans' names

Atlantic Ocean	oqyānus-e atlas	اقیانوس اطلس
Indian Ocean	oqyānus-e hend	اقیانوس هند
Pacific Ocean	oqyānus-e ārām	اقیانوس آرام
Arctic Ocean	oqyānus-e monjamed-e šomāli	اقیانوس منجمد شمالی

Black Sea	daryā-ye siyāh	دریای سیاه
Red Sea	daryā-ye sorx	دریای سرخ
Yellow Sea	daryā-ye zard	دریای زرد
White Sea	daryā-ye sefid	دریای سفید
Caspian Sea	daryā-ye xazar	دریای خزر
Dead Sea	daryā-ye morde	دریای مرده
Mediterranean Sea	daryā-ye meditarāne	دریای مدیترانه
Aegean Sea	daryā-ye eže	دریای اژه
Adriatic Sea	daryā-ye ādriyātik	دریای آدریاتیک
Arabian Sea	daryā-ye arab	دریای عرب
Sea of Japan	daryā-ye žāpon	دریای ژاپن
Bering Sea	daryā-ye brinq	دریای برینگ
South China Sea	daryā-ye čin-e jonubi	دریای چین جنوبی
Coral Sea	daryā-ye marjān	دریای مرجان
Tasman Sea	daryā-ye tās-emān	دریای تاسمان
Caribbean Sea	daryā-ye kārāib	دریای کارائیب
Barents Sea	daryā-ye barntz	دریای بارنتز
Kara Sea	daryā-ye kārā	دریای کارا
North Sea	daryā-ye šomāl	دریای شمال
Baltic Sea	daryā-ye bāltik	دریای بالتیک
Norwegian Sea	daryā-ye norvež	دریای نروژ

79. Mountains

mountain	kuh	کوه
mountain range	rešte-ye kuh	رشته کوه
mountain ridge	selsele-ye jebāl	سلسله جبال
summit, top	qolle	قله
peak	qolle	قله
foot (~ of the mountain)	dāmane-ye kuh	دامنۀ کوه
slope (mountainside)	šib	شیب
volcano	ātaš-fešān	آتشفشان
active volcano	ātaš-fešān-e fa'āl	آتش فشان فعال
dormant volcano	ātaš-fešān-e xāmuš	آتش فشان خاموش
eruption	favarān	فوران
crater	dahāne-ye ātašfešān	دهانۀ آتش فشان
magma	māgmā	ماگما
lava	godāze	گدازه
molten (~ lava)	godāxte	گداخته
canyon	tange	تنگه
gorge	darre-ye tang	دره تنگ

crevice	tange	تنگه
abyss (chasm)	partgāh	پرتگاه
pass, col	gozargāh	گذرگاه
plateau	falāt	فلات
cliff	saxre	صخره
hill	tappe	تپه
glacier	yaxčāl	یخچال
waterfall	ābšār	آبشار
geyser	češme-ye āb-e garm	چشمهٔ آب گرم
lake	daryāče	دریاچه
plain	jolge	جلگه
landscape	manzare	منظره
echo	en'ekās-e sowt	انعکاس صوت
alpinist	kuhnavard	کوهنورد
rock climber	saxre-ye navard	صخره نورد
to conquer (in climbing)	fath kardan	فتح کردن
climb (an easy ~)	so'ud	صعود

80. Mountains names

The Alps	ālp	آلپ
Mont Blanc	moan belān	مون بلان
The Pyrenees	pirene	پیرنه
The Carpathians	kuhhā-ye kārpāt	کوههای کارپات
The Ural Mountains	kuhe-i orāl	کوههای اورال
The Caucasus Mountains	qafqāz	قفقاز
Mount Elbrus	alborz	البرز
The Altai Mountains	āltāy	آلتای
The Tian Shan	tiyān šān	تیان شان
The Pamir Mountains	pāmir	پامیر
The Himalayas	himāliyā-vo	هیمالیا
Mount Everest	everest	اورست
The Andes	ānd	آند
Mount Kilimanjaro	kelimānjāro	کلیمانجارو

81. Rivers

river	rudxāne	رودخانه
spring (natural source)	češme	چشمه
riverbed (river channel)	bastar	بستر
basin (river valley)	howze	حوضه

to flow into ...	rixtan	ریختن
tributary	enše'āb	انشعاب
bank (of river)	sāhel	ساحل
current (stream)	jaryān	جریان
downstream (adv)	be samt-e pāin-e rudxāne	به سمت پائین رودخانه
upstream (adv)	be samt-e bālā-ye rudxāne	به سمت بالای رودخانه
inundation	seyl	سیل
flooding	toqyān	طغیان
to overflow (vi)	toqyān kardan	طغیان کردن
to flood (vt)	toqyān kardan	طغیان کردن
shallow (shoal)	tangāb	تنگاب
rapids	tondāb	تندآب
dam	sad	سد
canal	kānāl	کانال
reservoir (artificial lake)	maxzan-e āb	مخزن آب
sluice, lock	ābgir	آبگیر
water body (pond, etc.)	maxzan-e āb	مخزن آب
swamp (marshland)	bātlāq	باتلاق
bog, marsh	lajan zār	لجن زار
whirlpool	gerdāb	گرداب
stream (brook)	ravad	رود
drinking (ab. water)	āšāmidani	آشامیدنی
fresh (~ water)	širin	شیرین
ice	yax	یخ
to freeze over (ab. river, etc.)	yax bastan	یخ بستن

82. Rivers' names

Seine	sen	سن
Loire	lavār	لوآر
Thames	timz	تیمز
Rhine	rāyn	راین
Danube	dānub	دانوب
Volga	volgā	ولگا
Don	don	دن
Lena	lenā	لنا
Yellow River	rud-e zard	رود زرد
Yangtze	yāng tese	یانگ تسه
Mekong	mekung	مکونگ

Ganges	gong	گنگ
Nile River	neyl	نیل
Congo River	kongo	کنگو
Okavango River	okavango	اوکاوانگو
Zambezi River	zāmbezi	زامبزی
Limpopo River	rud-e limpupu	رود لیمپوپو
Mississippi River	mi si si pi	می سی سی پی

83. Forest

forest, wood	jangal	جنگل
forest (as adj)	jangali	جنگلی
thick forest	jangal-e anbuh	جنگل انبوه
grove	biše	بیشه
forest clearing	marqzār	مرغزار
thicket	biše-hā	بیشه ها
scrubland	bute zār	بوته زار
footpath (troddenpath)	kure-ye rāh	کوره راه
gully	darre	دره
tree	deraxt	درخت
leaf	barg	برگ
leaves (foliage)	šāx-o barg	شاخ و برگ
fall of leaves	barg rizi	برگ ریزی
to fall (ab. leaves)	rixtan	ریختن
top (of the tree)	nok	نوک
branch	šāxe	شاخه
bough	šāxe	شاخه
bud (on shrub, tree)	šokufe	شکوفه
needle (of pine tree)	suzan	سوزن
pine cone	maxrut-e kāj	مخروط کاج
hollow (in a tree)	surāx	سوراخ
nest	lāne	لانه
burrow (animal hole)	lāne	لانه
trunk	tane	تنه
root	riše	ریشه
bark	pust	پوست
moss	xaze	خزه
to uproot (remove trees or tree stumps)	rišekan kardan	ریشه کن کردن
to chop down	boridan	بریدن
to deforest (vt)	boridan	بریدن

tree stump	kande-ye deraxt	کندهٔ درخت
campfire	ātaš	آتش
forest fire	ātaš suzi	آتش سوزی
to extinguish (vt)	xāmuš kardan	خاموش کردن
forest ranger	jangal bān	جنگل بان
protection	mohāfezat	محافظت
to protect (~ nature)	mohāfezat kardan	محافظت کردن
poacher	šekārči-ye qeyr-e qānuni	شکارچی غیر قانونی
steel trap	tale	تله
to gather, to pick (vt)	čidan	چیدن
to lose one's way	gom šodan	گم شدن

84. Natural resources

natural resources	manābe-'e tabii	منابع طبیعی
minerals	mavādd-e ma'dani	مواد معدنی
deposits	tah nešast	ته نشست
field (e.g., oilfield)	meydān	میدان
to mine (extract)	estexrāj kardan	استخراج کردن
mining (extraction)	estexrāj	استخراج
ore	sang-e ma'dani	سنگ معدنی
mine (e.g., for coal)	ma'dan	معدن
shaft (mine ~)	ma'dan	معدن
miner	ma'danči	معدنچی
gas (natural ~)	gāz	گاز
gas pipeline	lule-ye gāz	لولهٔ گاز
oil (petroleum)	naft	نفت
oil pipeline	lule-ye naft	لولهٔ نفت
oil well	čāh-e naft	چاه نفت
derrick (tower)	dakal-e haffāri	دکل حفاری
tanker	tānker	تانکر
sand	šen	شن
limestone	sang-e āhak	سنگ آهک
gravel	sangrize	سنگریزه
peat	turb	تورب
clay	xāk-e ros	خاک رس
coal	zoqāl sang	زغال سنگ
iron (ore)	āhan	آهن
gold	talā	طلا
silver	noqre	نقره
nickel	nikel	نیکل
copper	mes	مس
zinc	ruy	روی

manganese	mangenez	منگنز
mercury	jive	جیوه
lead	sorb	سرب
mineral	mādde-ye ma'dani	مادهٔ معدنی
crystal	bolur	بلور
marble	marmar	مرمر
uranium	orāniyom	اورانیوم

85. Weather

weather	havā	هوا
weather forecast	piš bini havā	پیش بینی هوا
temperature	damā	دما
thermometer	damāsanj	دماسنج
barometer	havāsanj	هواسنج
humid (adj)	martub	مرطوب
humidity	rotubat	رطوبت
heat (extreme ~)	garmā	گرما
hot (torrid)	dāq	داغ
it's hot	havā xeyli garm ast	هوا خیلی گرم است
it's warm	havā garm ast	هوا گرم است
warm (moderately hot)	garm	گرم
it's cold	sard ast	سرد است
cold (adj)	sard	سرد
sun	āftāb	آفتاب
to shine (vi)	tābidan	تابیدن
sunny (day)	āftābi	آفتابی
to come up (vi)	tolu' kardan	طلوع کردن
to set (vi)	qorob kardan	غروب کردن
cloud	abr	ابر
cloudy (adj)	abri	ابری
rain cloud	abr-e bārānzā	ابر باران زا
somber (gloomy)	tire	تیره
rain	bārān	باران
it's raining	bārān mibārad	باران می بارد
rainy (~ day, weather)	bārāni	بارانی
to drizzle (vi)	nam-nam bāridan	نم نم باریدن
pouring rain	bārān šodid	باران شدید
downpour	ragbār	رگبار
heavy (e.g., ~ rain)	šadid	شدید
puddle	čāle	چاله

to get wet (in rain)	xis šodan	خیس شدن
fog (mist)	meh	مه
foggy	meh ālud	مه آلود
snow	barf	برف
it's snowing	barf mibārad	برف می بارد

86. Severe weather. Natural disasters

thunderstorm	tufān	طوفان
lightning (~ strike)	barq	برق
to flash (vi)	barq zadan	برق زدن
thunder	ra'd	رعد
to thunder (vi)	qorridan	غریدن
it's thundering	ra'd mizanad	رعد می زند
hail	tagarg	تگرگ
it's hailing	tagarg mibārad	تگرگ می بارد
to flood (vt)	toqyān kardan	طغیان کردن
flood, inundation	seyl	سیل
earthquake	zamin-larze	زمین لرزه
tremor, quake	tekān	تکان
epicenter	kānun-e zaminlarze	کانون زمین لرزه
eruption	favarān	فوران
lava	godāze	گدازه
twister, tornado	gerdbād	گردباد
typhoon	tufān	طوفان
hurricane	tufān	طوفان
storm	tufān	طوفان
tsunami	sonāmi	سونامی
cyclone	gerdbād	گردباد
bad weather	havā-ye bad	هوای بد
fire (accident)	ātaš suzi	آتش سوزی
disaster	balā-ye tabi'i	بلای طبیعی
meteorite	sang-e āsmāni	سنگ آسمانی
avalanche	bahman	بهمن
snowslide	bahman	بهمن
blizzard	kulāk	کولاک
snowstorm	barf-o burān	برف و بوران

FAUNA

87. Mammals. Predators

predator	heyvān-e darande	حیوان درنده
tiger	bebar	ببر
lion	šir	شیر
wolf	gorg	گرگ
fox	rubāh	روباه
jaguar	jagvār	جگوار
leopard	palang	پلنگ
cheetah	yuzpalang	یوزپلنگ
black panther	palang-e siyāh	پلنگ سیاه
puma	yuzpalang	یوزپلنگ
snow leopard	palang-e barfi	پلنگ برفی
lynx	siyāh guš	سیاه گوش
coyote	gorg-e sahrāyi	گرگ صحرایی
jackal	šoqāl	شغال
hyena	kaftār	کفتار

88. Wild animals

animal	heyvān	حیوان
beast (animal)	heyvān	حیوان
squirrel	sanjāb	سنجاب
hedgehog	xārpošt	خارپشت
hare	xarguš	خرگوش
rabbit	xarguš	خرگوش
badger	gurkan	گورکن
raccoon	rākon	راکون
hamster	muš-e bozorg	موش بزرگ
marmot	muš-e xormā-ye kuhi	موش خرمای کوهی
mole	muš-e kur	موش کور
mouse	muš	موش
rat	muš-e sahrāyi	موش صحرایی
bat	xoffāš	خفاش
ermine	qāqom	قاقم
sable	samur	سمور

marten	samur	سمور
weasel	rāsu	راسو
mink	tire-ye rāsu	تیره راسو

| beaver | sag-e ābi | سگ آبی |
| otter | samur ābi | سمور آبی |

horse	asb	اسب
moose	gavazn	گوزن
deer	āhu	آهو
camel	šotor	شتر

bison	gāvmiš	گاومیش
aurochs	gāv miš	گاو میش
buffalo	bufālo	بوفالو

zebra	gurexar	گورخر
antelope	boz-e kuhi	بز کوهی
roe deer	šukā	شوکا
fallow deer	qazāl	غزال
chamois	boz-e kuhi	بز کوهی
wild boar	gorāz	گراز

whale	nahang	نهنگ
seal	fak	فک
walrus	širmāhi	شیرماهی
fur seal	gorbe-ye ābi	گربهٔ آبی
dolphin	delfin	دلفین

bear	xers	خرس
polar bear	xers-e sefid	خرس سفید
panda	pāndā	پاندا

monkey	meymun	میمون
chimpanzee	šampānze	شمپانزه
orangutan	orāngutān	اورانگتان
gorilla	guril	گوریل
macaque	mākāk	ماکاک
gibbon	gibon	گیبون

elephant	fil	فیل
rhinoceros	kargadan	کرگدن
giraffe	zarrāfe	زرافه
hippopotamus	asb-e ābi	اسب آبی

| kangaroo | kāngoro | کانگورو |
| koala (bear) | kovālā | کوالا |

mongoose	xadang	خدنگ
chinchilla	čin čila	چین چیلا
skunk	rāsu-ye badbu	راسوی بدبو
porcupine	taši	تشی

89. Domestic animals

cat	gorbe	گربه
tomcat	gorbe-ye nar	گربهٔ نر
dog	sag	سگ
horse	asb	اسب
stallion (male horse)	asb-e nar	اسب نر
mare	mādiyān	مادیان
cow	gāv	گاو
bull	gāv-e nar	گاو نر
ox	gāv-e axte	گاو اخته
sheep (ewe)	gusfand	گوسفند
ram	gusfand-e nar	گوسفند نر
goat	boz-e mādde	بز ماده
billy goat, he-goat	boz-e nar	بز نر
donkey	xar	خر
mule	qāter	قاطر
pig, hog	xuk	خوک
piglet	bače-ye xuk	بچهٔ خوک
rabbit	xarguš	خرگوش
hen (chicken)	morq	مرغ
rooster	xorus	خروس
duck	ordak	اردک
drake	ordak-e nar	اردک نر
goose	qāz	غاز
tom turkey, gobbler	buqalamun-e nar	بوقلمون نر
turkey (hen)	buqalamun-e māde	بوقلمون ماده
domestic animals	heyvānāt-e ahli	حیوانات اهلی
tame (e.g., ~ hamster)	ahli	اهلی
to tame (vt)	rām kardan	رام کردن
to breed (vt)	parvareš dādan	پرورش دادن
farm	mazrae	مزرعه
poultry	morq-e xānegi	مرغ خانگی
cattle	dām	دام
herd (cattle)	galle	گله
stable	establ	اصطبل
pigpen	āqol xuk	آغل خوک
cowshed	āqol gāv	آغل گاو
rabbit hutch	lanye xarguš	لانه خرگوش
hen house	morq dāni	مرغ دانی

90. Birds

bird	parande	پرنده
pigeon	kabutar	کبوتر
sparrow	gonješk	گنجشک
tit (great tit)	morq-e zanburxār	مرغ زنبورخوار
magpie	zāqi	زاغی
raven	kalāq-e siyāh	کلاغ سیاه
crow	kalāq	کلاغ
jackdaw	zāq	زاغ
rook	kalāq-e siyāh	کلاغ سیاه
duck	ordak	اردک
goose	qāz	غاز
pheasant	qarqāvol	قرقاول
eagle	oqāb	عقاب
hawk	qerqi	قرقی
falcon	šāhin	شاهین
vulture	karkas	کرکس
condor (Andean ~)	karkas-e emrikāyi	کرکس امریکایی
swan	qu	قو
crane	dornā	درنا
stork	lak lak	لک لک
parrot	tuti	طوطی
hummingbird	morq-e magas-e xār	مرغ مگس خوار
peacock	tāvus	طاووس
ostrich	šotormorq	شترمرغ
heron	havāsil	حواصیل
flamingo	felāmingo	فلامینگو
pelican	pelikān	پلیکان
nightingale	bolbol	بلبل
swallow	parastu	پرستو
thrush	bāstarak	باسترک
song thrush	torqe	طرقه
blackbird	tukā-ye siyāh	توکای سیاه
swift	bādxorak	بادخورک
lark	čakāvak	چکاوک
quail	belderčin	بلدرچین
woodpecker	dārkub	دارکوب
cuckoo	fāxte	فاخته
owl	joqd	جغد
eagle owl	šāh buf	شاه بوف

wood grouse	siāh xorus	سیاه خروس
black grouse	siāh xorus-e jangali	سیاه خروس جنگلی
partridge	kabk	کبک

starling	sār	سار
canary	qanāri	قناری
hazel grouse	siyāh xorus-e fandoqi	سیاه خروس فندقی
chaffinch	sehre-ye jangali	سهره جنگلی
bullfinch	sohre sar-e siyāh	سهره سر سیاه

seagull	morq-e daryāyi	مرغ دریایی
albatross	morq-e daryāyi	مرغ دریایی
penguin	pangoan	پنگوئن

91. Fish. Marine animals

bream	māhi-ye sim	ماهی سیم
carp	kapur	کپور
perch	māhi-e luti	ماهی لوتی
catfish	gorbe-ye māhi	گربه ماهی
pike	ordak māhi	اردک ماهی

| salmon | māhi-ye salemon | ماهی سالمون |
| sturgeon | māhi-ye xāviār | ماهی خاویار |

herring	māhi-ye šur	ماهی شور
Atlantic salmon	sālmon-e atlāntik	سالمون اتلانتیک
mackerel	māhi-ye esqumeri	ماهی اسقومری
flatfish	sofre māhi	سفره ماهی

zander, pike perch	suf	سوف
cod	māhi-ye rowqan	ماهی روغن
tuna	tan māhi	تن ماهی
trout	māhi-ye qezelālā	ماهی قزل آلا

eel	mārmāhi	مارماهی
electric ray	partomahiye barqi	پرتوماهی برقی
moray eel	mārmāhi	مارماهی
piranha	pirānā	پیرانا

shark	kuse-ye māhi	کوسه ماهی
dolphin	delfin	دلفین
whale	nahang	نهنگ

crab	xarčang	خرچنگ
jellyfish	arus-e daryāyi	عروس دریایی
octopus	hašt pā	هشت پا

| starfish | setāre-ye daryāyi | ستاره دریایی |
| sea urchin | xārpošt-e daryāyi | خارپشت دریایی |

seahorse	asb-e daryāyi	اسب دریایی
oyster	sadaf-e xorāki	صدف خوراکی
shrimp	meygu	میگو
lobster	xarčang-e daryāyi	خرچنگ دریایی
spiny lobster	xarčang-e xārdār	خرچنگ خاردار

92. Amphibians. Reptiles

snake	mār	مار
venomous (snake)	sammi	سمی
viper	af'i	افعی
cobra	kobrā	کبرا
python	mār-e pinton	مار پیتون
boa	mār-e bwa	مار بوا
grass snake	mār-e čaman	مار چمن
rattle snake	mār-e zangi	مار زنگی
anaconda	mār-e ānākondā	مار آناکوندا
lizard	susmār	سوسمار
iguana	susmār-e deraxti	سوسمار درختی
monitor lizard	bozmajje	بزمجه
salamander	samandar	سمندر
chameleon	āftāb-parast	آفتاب پرست
scorpion	aqrab	عقرب
turtle	lāk pošt	لاک پشت
frog	qurbāqe	قورباغه
toad	vazaq	وزغ
crocodile	temsāh	تمساح

93. Insects

insect, bug	hašare	حشره
butterfly	parvāne	پروانه
ant	murče	مورچه
fly	magas	مگس
mosquito	paše	پشه
beetle	susk	سوسک
wasp	zanbur	زنبور
bee	zanbur-e asal	زنبور عسل
bumblebee	xar zanbur	خرزنبور
gadfly (botfly)	xarmagas	خرمگس
spider	ankabut	عنکبوت
spiderweb	tār-e ankabut	تارعنکبوت

dragonfly	sanjāqak	سنجاقک
grasshopper	malax	ملخ
moth (night butterfly)	bid	بید
cockroach	susk	سوسک
tick	kane	کنه
flea	kak	کک
midge	paše-ye rize	پشه ریزه
locust	malax	ملخ
snail	halazun	حلزون
cricket	jirjirak	جیرجیرک
lightning bug	kerm-e šab-tāb	کرم شب تاب
ladybug	kafšduzak	کفشدوزک
cockchafer	susk bāldār	سوسک بالدار
leech	zālu	زالو
caterpillar	kerm-e abrišam	کرم ابریشم
earthworm	kerm	کرم
larva	lārv	لارو

FLORA

94. Trees

tree	deraxt	درخت
deciduous (adj)	barg riz	برگ ریز
coniferous (adj)	maxrutiyān	مخروطیان
evergreen (adj)	hamiše sabz	همیشه سبز
apple tree	deraxt-e sib	درخت سیب
pear tree	golābi	گلابی
sweet cherry tree	gilās	گیلاس
sour cherry tree	ālbālu	آلبالو
plum tree	ālu	آلو
birch	tus	توس
oak	balut	بلوط
linden tree	zirfun	زیرفین
aspen	senowbar-e larzān	صنوبر لرزان
maple	afrā	افرا
spruce	senowbar	صنوبر
pine	kāj	کاج
larch	senowbar-e ārāste	صنوبر آراسته
fir tree	šāh deraxt	شاه درخت
cedar	sedr	سدر
poplar	sepidār	سپیدار
rowan	zabān gonješk-e kuhi	زبان گنجشک کوهی
willow	bid	بید
alder	tuskā	توسکا
beech	rāš	راش
elm	nārvan-e qermez	نارون قرمز
ash (tree)	zabān-e gonješk	زبان گنجشک
chestnut	šāh balut	شاه بلوط
magnolia	māgnoliyā	ماگنولیا
palm tree	naxl	نخل
cypress	sarv	سرو
mangrove	karnā	کرنا
baobab	bāobāb	بائوباب
eucalyptus	okaliptus	اوکالیپتوس
sequoia	sorx-e čub	سرخ چوب

95. Shrubs

bush	bute	بوته
shrub	bute zār	بوته زار
grapevine	angur	انگور
vineyard	tākestān	تاکستان
raspberry bush	tamešk	تمشک
blackcurrant bush	angur-e farangi-ye siyāh	انگور فرنگی سیاه
redcurrant bush	angur-e farangi-ye sorx	انگور فرنگی سرخ
gooseberry bush	angur-e farangi	انگور فرنگی
acacia	aqāqiyā	اقاقیا
barberry	zerešk	زرشک
jasmine	yāsaman	یاسمن
juniper	ardaj	اردج
rosebush	bute-ye gol-e mohammadi	بوتهٔ گل محمدی
dog rose	nastaran	نسترن

96. Fruits. Berries

fruit	mive	میوه
fruits	mive jāt	میوه جات
apple	sib	سیب
pear	golābi	گلابی
plum	ālu	آلو
strawberry (garden ~)	tut-e farangi	توت فرنگی
sour cherry	ālbālu	آلبالو
sweet cherry	gilās	گیلاس
grape	angur	انگور
raspberry	tamešk	تمشک
blackcurrant	angur-e farangi-ye siyāh	انگور فرنگی سیاه
redcurrant	angur-e farangi-ye sorx	انگور فرنگی سرخ
gooseberry	angur-e farangi	انگور فرنگی
cranberry	nārdānak-e vahši	ناردانک وحشی
orange	porteqāl	پرتقال
mandarin	nārengi	نارنگی
pineapple	ānānās	آناناس
banana	mowz	موز
date	xormā	خرما
lemon	limu	لیمو
apricot	zardālu	زردآلو

peach	holu	هلو
kiwi	kivi	کیوی
grapefruit	gerip forut	گریپ فوروت
berry	mive-ye butei	میوهٔ بوته ای
berries	mivehā-ye butei	میوه های بوته ای
cowberry	tut-e farangi-ye jangali	توت فرنگی جنگلی
wild strawberry	zoqāl axte	زغال اخته
bilberry	zoqāl axte	زغال اخته

97. Flowers. Plants

flower	gol	گل
bouquet (of flowers)	daste-ye gol	دسته گل
rose (flower)	gol-e sorx	گل سرخ
tulip	lāle	لاله
carnation	mixak	میخک
gladiolus	susan-e sefid	سوسن سفید
cornflower	gol-e gandom	گل گندم
harebell	gol-e estekāni	گل استکانی
dandelion	gol-e qāsedak	گل قاصدک
camomile	bābune	بابونه
aloe	oloviye	آلوئه
cactus	kāktus	کاکتوس
rubber plant, ficus	fikus	فیکوس
lily	susan	سوسن
geranium	gol-e šam‘dāni	گل شمعدانی
hyacinth	sonbol	سنبل
mimosa	mimosā	میموسا
narcissus	narges	نرگس
nasturtium	gol-e lādan	گل لادن
orchid	orkide	ارکیده
peony	gol-e ašrafi	گل اشرفی
violet	banafše	بنفشه
pansy	banafše-ye farangi	بنفشه فرنگی
forget-me-not	gol-e farāmuš-am makon	گل فراموشم مکن
daisy	gol-e morvārid	گل مروارید
poppy	xašxāš	خشخاش
hemp	šāh dāne	شاه دانه
mint	na‘nā‘	نعناع
lily of the valley	muge	موگه
snowdrop	gol-e barfi	گل برفی

nettle	gazane	گزنه
sorrel	toršak	ترشک
water lily	nilufar-e abi	نیلوفر آبی
fern	saraxs	سرخس
lichen	golesang	گلسنگ
greenhouse (tropical ~)	golxāne	گلخانه
lawn	čaman	چمن
flowerbed	baqče-ye gol	باغچه گل
plant	giyāh	گیاه
grass	alaf	علف
blade of grass	alaf	علف
leaf	barg	برگ
petal	golbarg	گلبرگ
stem	sāqe	ساقه
tuber	riše	ریشه
young plant (shoot)	javāne	جوانه
thorn	xār	خار
to blossom (vi)	gol kardan	گل کردن
to fade, to wither	pažmorde šodan	پژمرده شدن
smell (odor)	bu	بو
to cut (flowers)	boridan	بریدن
to pick (a flower)	kandan	کندن

98. Cereals, grains

grain	dāne	دانه
cereal crops	qallāt	غلات
ear (of barley, etc.)	xuše	خوشه
wheat	gandom	گندم
rye	čāvdār	چاودار
oats	jow-e sahrāyi	جو صحرایی
millet	arzan	ارزن
barley	jow	جو
corn	zorrat	ذرت
rice	berenj	برنج
buckwheat	gandom-e siyāh	گندم سیاه
pea plant	noxod	نخود
kidney bean	lubiyā qermez	لوبیا قرمز
soy	sowyā	سویا
lentil	adas	عدس
beans (pulse crops)	lubiyā	لوبیا

COUNTRIES OF THE WORLD

99. Countries. Part 1

Afghanistan	afqānestān	افغانستان
Albania	ālbāni	آلبانی
Argentina	āržāntin	آرژانتین
Armenia	armanestān	ارمنستان
Australia	ostorāliyā	استرالیا
Austria	otriš	اتریش
Azerbaijan	āzarbāyjān	آذربایجان
The Bahamas	bāhāmā	باهاما
Bangladesh	bangelādeš	بنگلادش
Belarus	belārus	بلاروس
Belgium	belžik	بلژیک
Bolivia	bulivi	بولیوی
Bosnia and Herzegovina	bosni-yo herzogovin	بوسنی وهرزگوین
Brazil	berezil	برزیل
Bulgaria	bolqārestān	بلغارستان
Cambodia	kāmboj	کامبوج
Canada	kānādā	کانادا
Chile	šhili	شیلی
China	čin	چین
Colombia	kolombiyā	کلمبیا
Croatia	korovāsi	کرواسی
Cuba	kubā	کوبا
Cyprus	qebres	قبرس
Czech Republic	jomhuri-ye ček	جمهوری چک
Denmark	dānmārk	دانمارک
Dominican Republic	jomhuri-ye dominikan	جمهوری دومینیکن
Ecuador	ekvādor	اکوادور
Egypt	mesr	مصر
England	engelestān	انگلستان
Estonia	estoni	استونی
Finland	fanlānd	فنلاند
France	farānse	فرانسه
French Polynesia	polinezi-ye farānse	پلینزی فرانسه
Georgia	gorjestān	گرجستان
Germany	ālmān	آلمان
Ghana	qanā	غنا
Great Britain	beritāniyā-ye kabir	بریتانیای کبیر
Greece	yunān	یونان

| Haiti | hāiti | هائیتی |
| Hungary | majārestān | مجارستان |

100. Countries. Part 2

Iceland	island	ایسلند
India	hendustān	هندوستان
Indonesia	andonezi	اندونزی
Iran	irān	ایران
Iraq	arāq	عراق
Ireland	irland	ایرلند
Israel	esrāil	اسرائیل
Italy	itāliyā	ایتالیا

Jamaica	jāmāikā	جامائیکا
Japan	žāpon	ژاپن
Jordan	ordon	اردن
Kazakhstan	qazzāqestān	قزاقستان
Kenya	keniyā	کنیا
Kirghizia	qerqizestān	قرقیزستان
Kuwait	koveyt	کویت

Laos	lāus	لائوس
Latvia	letuni	لتونی
Lebanon	lobnān	لبنان
Libya	libi	لیبی
Liechtenstein	lixteneštāyn	لیختن‌اشتاین
Lithuania	litvāni	لیتوانی
Luxembourg	lokzāmborg	لوکزامبورگ

Macedonia (Republic of ~)	jomhuri-ye maqduniye	جمهوری مقدونیه
Madagascar	mādāgāskār	ماداگاسکار
Malaysia	mālezi	مالزی
Malta	mālt	مالت
Mexico	mekzik	مکزیک
Moldova, Moldavia	moldāvi	مولداوی

Monaco	monāko	موناکو
Mongolia	moqolestān	مغولستان
Montenegro	montenegro	مونته‌نگرو

| Morocco | marākeš | مراکش |
| Myanmar | miyānmār | میانمار |

Namibia	nāmibiyā	نامیبیا
Nepal	nepāl	نپال
Netherlands	holand	هلند
New Zealand	niyuzland	نیوزلند
North Korea	kare-ye šomāli	کرهٔ شمالی
Norway	norvež	نروژ

101. Countries. Part 3

Pakistan	pākestān	پاکستان
Palestine	felestin	فلسطین
Panama	pānāmā	پاناما
Paraguay	pārāgue	پاراگوئه
Peru	porov	پرو
Poland	lahestān	لهستان
Portugal	porteqāl	پرتغال
Romania	romāni	رومانی
Russia	rusiye	روسیه
Saudi Arabia	arabestān-e so'udi	عربستان سعودی
Scotland	eskātland	اسکاتلند
Senegal	senegāl	سنگال
Serbia	serbestān	صربستان
Slovakia	eslovāki	اسلواکی
Slovenia	eslovoni	اسلوونی
South Africa	jomhuri-ye āfriqā-ye jonubi	جمهوری آفریقای جنوبی
South Korea	kare-ye jonubi	کرهٔ جنوبی
Spain	espāniyā	اسپانیا
Suriname	surinām	سورینام
Sweden	sued	سوئد
Switzerland	suis	سوئیس
Syria	suriye	سوریه
Taiwan	tāyvān	تایوان
Tajikistan	tājikestān	تاجیکستان
Tanzania	tānzāniyā	تانزانیا
Tasmania	tāsmāni	تاسمانی
Thailand	tāyland	تایلند
Tunisia	tunes	تونس
Turkey	torkiye	ترکیه
Turkmenistan	torkamanestān	ترکمنستان
Ukraine	okrāyn	اوکراین
United Arab Emirates	emārāt-e mottahede-ye arabi	امارات متحده عربی
United States of America	eyālāt-e mottahede-ye emrikā	ایالات متحدهٔ امریکا
Uruguay	orogue	اوروگوئه
Uzbekistan	ozbakestān	ازبکستان
Vatican	vātikān	واتیکان
Venezuela	venezuelā	ونزوئلا
Vietnam	viyetnām	ویتنام
Zanzibar	zangbār	زنگبار